The Cold War

A FOCUS BOOK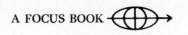

THE
COLD WAR

by Morrie Helitzer

FRANKLIN WATTS
NEW YORK|LONDON|1977

FOR CYNTHIA, IRENE, JONATHAN

Photographs courtesy of: United Press International: pp. 2, 29, 36, 67 (top and bottom), 70, 82; NATO: p. 11; United Nations: p. 24 (top and bottom); Associated Press: p. 43; U.S. Army, p. 53; NASA: p. 86.

Library of Congress Cataloging in Publication Data

Helitzer, Morrie.
    The cold war.

    (A Focus book)
    Bibliography: p.
    Includes index.
    SUMMARY: Examines the origins and political implications of the power struggle between the United States and the Soviet Union since the end of World War II.
    1. World politics—1945- —Juvenile literature.
[1. World politics] I. Title.
D842.H43   327′.09′045   77-4668
ISBN 0-531-02464-4

Contents

Introduction

In the curious way that books are put together, the author writes the Introduction last. It allows for an afterthought that may not fit into the chapters proper.

As I reflect on a period that is distant or unknown to some readers, I am led to a curious conclusion about the Cold War. It is a personal opinion rather than a provable fact, but this is what it comes to: After World War II, the United States and the Soviet Union were bound to do battle. If they had not fought a Cold War, it could have been a hot one, touched off by accident or design, but with a good probability of turning into a nuclear nightmare.

Why do I think a war was inevitable? Because in 1945 the United States and the USSR were the only two global powers on earth. They were bound to meet, compete, bump, and bully each other not in one or two geographic areas, but in dozens of places on the planet and finally in space itself. The name of the game was power, and power means periodic use of force.

From that point of view, we were lucky to get away with a Cold War.

Finally, a word about historical treatment. For some years, most American historians wrote as though the Russians alone were to blame for the Cold War. In the 1960s, a "revisionist" school began to find greater fault with the United States. In this book, I have tried to avoid placing blame. However, I have made judgments about the political systems of the two superpowers and how those differing systems affect governmental actions at home and abroad.

Morrie Helitzer

The historic meeting of American and Soviet soldiers on the bridge over the Elbe in April 1945.

Meeting on the Elbe

They met on the River Elbe with cries of:

"Amerikansky."

"Russky."

"Stalin."

"Roosevelt."

"Churchill."

"Tovarisch."

"Chevrolet. Studebaker."

GI Joe and Soviet Ivan joined hands on April 25, 1945 in the middle of ruined Germany, whose rulers had boasted of a thousand-year reign for the Third Reich. In Europe, World War II was nearing a close.

But even the carefully planned linkup of the two great armies from the East and West had been "snafued" (*S*ituation *N*ormal *A*ll *F*ouled *U*p) with one American patrol disobeying its orders and another coming under Russian fire in its eagerness to make contact. As the Soviets and Americans shook hands, bear-hugged, swapped cigarettes, and drank toasts of vodka and whiskey, none of the details seemed important.

For the Soviets, who had been fighting for nearly four years, mostly on their native soil, the war had taken a terrible toll. Some ten million soldiers and civilians had died, leaving a wound on the nation that would take more than a generation to heal. The destruction of their factories and equipment was equally catastrophic. In comparison with the United States, whose economy had been pushed into high gear by the war, the Union of Soviet Socialist Republics had lost ground. The slow, hard

climb from an agricultural state to a modern industrialized one had been stopped in its tracks.

In the years after the war, the loss of people and industrial capacity was a constant prod for Soviet leaders. Their fear that the West might try to take advantage of their weakness made them rigid in seeking control over the countries on their borders. This went to the point of Russia reducing them to satellites. At the same time, the Soviets kept large numbers of men under arms, after the United States and Britain had greatly reduced their armies, navies, and air forces. The shadow of a very large, combat-ready force in the East made the United States skeptical of the USSR's peaceful intentions. It also cost Soviet industry and agriculture sorely needed manpower.

The third great victor of World War II, the United Kingdom (Great Britain, as that country is also called) had been at war since September 3, 1939, the longest period among the Western Allies. Although the British Isles were never invaded, its cities had been pummeled by German bombers. The loss of manpower, empire, and energy toppled it from the ranks of the superpowers.

Two weeks before the U.S.-Soviet linkup on April 25, advance units of the U.S. Ninth Army were within a one-day dash up the Autobahn to Berlin, but were ordered to stay put. The decision was based on political not military grounds. As late as the middle of March 1945, the Supreme Allied Commander, General of the Army Dwight D. Eisenhower, thought the Russians would get to Berlin first because they were much closer. Under the circumstances, Eisenhower believed it would reassure Generalissimo Stalin if the Western Allies did not turn the capture of Berlin into a race. Stalin was already highly suspicious that

the United States and Britain were negotiating secretly for a separate surrender of Germany. Maybe Stalin would be convinced of the West's goodwill if Berlin were left to the Red Army. Winston Churchill, the British prime minister, argued for getting to Berlin first. It was a great military, political, and psychological prize, he insisted, well worth a strong effort in order to run up the American and British flags. But Roosevelt overruled him.

Virtually at the moment of Roosevelt's death on April 12, 1945, the military picture changed dramatically. Americans and Russians were now about the same distance from the German capital. Faced with lighter resistance, the American field commanders were sure they could drive up the Autobahn, the German superhighway, to the suburbs of Berlin within twenty-four hours. The matter was put to President Truman. Just sworn into office, he accepted General Eisenhower's statement that Berlin had no value militarily. The American armies were ordered to hold on the Elbe, allowing the Russians to proceed with their assault on the city.

By standing aside on Berlin, the Western powers did not increase Stalin's trust. Diplomatic experts on the Soviet Union—or Kremlinologists as they are called—said it just puzzled the Soviet dictator as to what the Americans were really after. When power and the upper hand were at stake, friendship, generosity, and fairness did not enter into Stalin's calculations.

Berlin fell to the Russians after a bloody battle. Hitler committed suicide. The crushed German armies surrendered, and on May 7, 1945 the war in Europe was over. Under an agreement among the USSR, the United States, and United Kingdom, to which France was later made a party, Germany was divided

EUROPE DURING THE COLD WAR

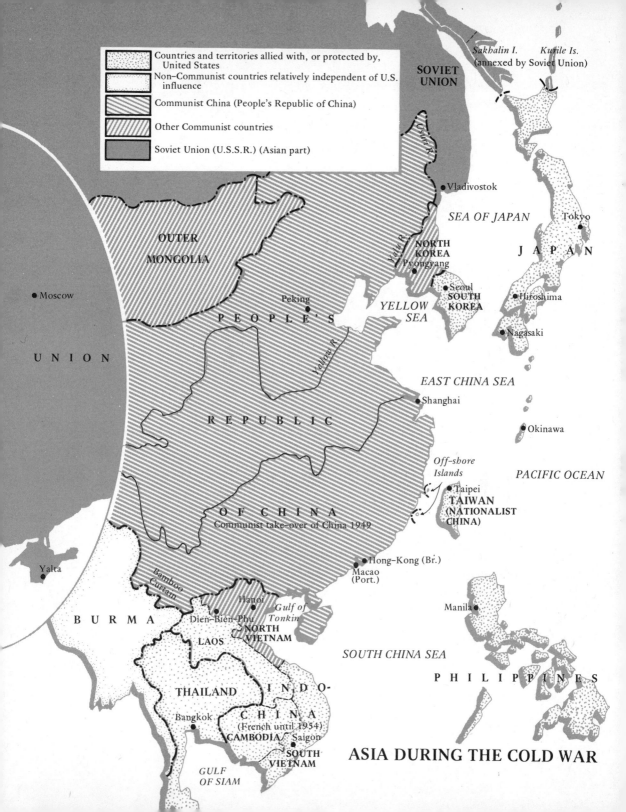

Legend:

- Countries and territories allied with, or protected by, United States
- Non-Communist countries relatively independent of U.S. influence
- Communist China (People's Republic of China)
- Other Communist countries
- Soviet Union (U.S.S.R.) (Asian part)

Sakhalin I. *Kurile Is.*
(annexed by Soviet Union)

SOVIET
UNION

Vladivostok

SEA OF JAPAN

Tokyo

Ussur R.

NORTH
KOREA
Pyongyang

Seoul
SOUTH
KOREA

Yalu R.

J A P A N

Hiroshima

*YELLOW
SEA*

Nagasaki

•Moscow

OUTER
MONGOLIA

Peking•

P E O P L E ' S

EAST CHINA SEA

Yellow R.

R E P U B L I C

Shanghai

Okinawa

U N I O N

*Off-shore
Islands*

PACIFIC OCEAN

O F   C H I N A
Communist take-over of China 1949

•Taipei
TAIWAN
(NATIONALIST
CHINA)

•Yalta

Hong-Kong (Br.)
Macao
(Port.)

*Bamboo
Curtain*

Hanoi•
*Gulf of
Tonkin*

Manila•

B U R M A

Dien-Bien-Phu
NORTH
VIETNAM

LAOS

SOUTH CHINA SEA

P H I L I P P I N E S

THAILAND

I N D O -

C H I N A

Bangkok•

(French until 1954)
CAMBODIA Saigon•

SOUTH
VIETNAM

*GULF
OF SIAM*

ASIA DURING THE COLD WAR

into four zones of occupation. The city of Berlin, deep within the Soviet zone of Germany, also was divided into four sectors, each administered by a commandant of a victorious power.

When the Western Allies drove into Berlin to assume their commands, there were ceremonies, salutes, and handshakes once more. But in small ways, and then more clearly, the Soviets pointed out that the Western powers were in Berlin by special permission, not by absolute right. Instead of being a symbol of joint rule, Berlin increasingly became a contested prize. As much as any spot on earth, it was turned into a focus of rivalries and confrontations between the United States and the Soviet Union. A crisis between the two superpowers anywhere became a signal for military forces in Berlin to go on alert. And on more than one occasion, the tension grew to a point where both countries moved for their nuclear and thermonuclear weapons.

Thirty years after soldiers of the two armies met on the River Elbe, a Soviet colonel and an American general shook hands once more—this time in space, 136 miles (219 kilometers) above the earth. The linkup of a Soviet cosmonaut and an American astronaut was the final act in another rivalry, this time to put the first man on the moon. The Americans won, but it was not a rerun of Berlin and Germany. Both nations had decided not to extend their military competition into space. Each nation sent its crew aloft in 1975 in its own spaceship to meet not in a "no-man's-land" but in an "everyone's land." It was part of what was hailed as the spirit of détente.

Between those two sets of handshakes, through countless encounters, sometimes friendly, more often warlike, the United States and USSR pursued with religious enthusiasm the goal of being number one. The weapons of destruction available to each were unparalleled. Each had and still has the ability to annihilate the other completely, together with virtually every other nation on earth. We can guess that, during those thirty years, had one been able to destroy the other without being destroyed also, the safety catch on the atomic gun would have been fired.

But it never happened. Each power sent out its troops, planes, tanks, and infantry, fought battles, and suffered casualties without throwing the big one, or directly engaging the other. In Korea and in Vietnam, the United States fought two of its bitterest and most frustrating wars. Although Soviet supplies and support weighed in on the Communist side and their pilots flew missions in Korea, their troops did not take the field. Thus in 1950, when the Cold War suddenly turned hot, it did not follow the scripts laid out by the political pundits or the generals.

In this book, we will look at the beginnings of the Cold War and consider whether it has ended, or just gone quiet. But first, think of the term "Cold War." Is it a new phase in international relations, or an updated version of "no-war, no-peace" periods of the past? In the seventeenth, eighteenth, and nineteenth centuries, European nations used something between war and peace as a way of marking time until ready for the next encounter. For the United States of America, the period between the end of the American Revolution in 1783 and the start of the War of 1812 was very much a no-war, no-peace era with Britain.

It does not matter whether the Cold War is a true "first." It is fascinating to look more closely at how two nations with unprecedented power have managed to live side by side for more than three decades; at how it affected their relations with each other, with friends and enemies, and what it did to the lives of their own citizens. This book focuses chiefly on the United States, but makes an effort to understand events, actions, and policies in the Soviet Union as well.

[9]

Seeds of the Cold War

How did this strange war between two victorious allies begin? Berlin, by itself, certainly was not sufficient cause; nor, for that matter, was Germany. Both the United States and the USSR had ample living space for their populations. Neither sought the territory of the other. Indeed, a problem for the Soviet Union was finding pioneers for the vast frontier areas in the Asian portion of the country. Lacking volunteers, the solution was to force people to work. As for natural resources, both were amply blessed. Finally, while the governments had not been friendly, there was an absence of the deep-seated hatreds among their people such as those that existed between Germans and French, Greeks and Turks, or between India's Hindus and Muslims.

Could the Cold War be traced to an ambitious leader who saw himself as another Alexander the Great, Caesar, or Napoleon? On that score, critics of Franklin D. Roosevelt, the first American president to serve more than two terms, or of Josef Stalin, for twenty-five years the dictator of his nation, might say yes. But neither singlehandedly led his country into the Cold War. And President Roosevelt's successor, Truman, who was more blamed for the Cold War than Roosevelt, was certainly not a would-be twentieth-century emperor.

In fact, the peoples of the United States and the Union of Soviet Socialist Republics knew relatively little of each other. The Russians who had emigrated in great waves to the United States in the nineteenth and early twentieth centuries seemed as different from the Bolsheviks as modern man was from the

The "Big Three" pose during their meeting at Potsdam: left to right, Churchill, Truman, and Stalin.

Neanderthal. Those pre-1917 Russian and Eastern European immigrants belonged to the tradition of newcomers who gratefully found America to be "land of the free, home of the brave." As for the Bolsheviks, to the extent that Americans knew or cared about them, they frequently pictured cartoonlike characters in long coats and beards with lighted bombs in their hands.

For the Soviet leaders, the West was a shifting combination of hostile powers. It included Germany, the nations of the old Austro-Hungarian empire, Britain, France, Italy and, off to the east, an equally belligerent Japan. An expeditionary force drawn from the European countries, as well as from the United States, had invaded the newly formed Soviet Union in 1918–19 to help the "White Russians" overthrow Lenin's "Red Russians." The expeditionary force failed and withdrew. In the process, however, Finland and the Baltic nations of Latvia, Lithuania, and Estonia became independent, and Poland regained her sovereignty. For the new Soviet leaders, the expeditionary force was a continuation of centuries of foreign hostility aimed at humbling Mother Russia. Only by the overthrow of capitalism and the establishment of Communist governments in other countries would the Soviet Union be safe, Lenin believed.

Like an echo caught between mountains, the actions of the United States and the USSR boomed back at the other. The revolutionary spirit of the Communists frightened the Americans. Bolshevik shouts for the workers to arise helped trigger a series of raids and arrests by the U.S. attorney general in the early 1920s. Signs of the "Red menace" could be found everywhere for those intent on finding them. The trial, conviction, and execution in the 1920s of two Italian revolutionaries accused of bank robbery and murder in Massachusetts gained international attention. The admissions of Sacco and Vanzetti that they were anarchists seemed to weigh more heavily against the two immigrants than the crimes with which they were charged. The Sacco-Vanzetti case captured in a nutshell the fears, confusion, and excessive reaction triggered by the term *international Communist conspiracy*. Nevertheless, during the same 1920s Herbert Hoover, later to be president of the United States, organized a huge American food plan. It fed millions of Europeans and saved countless thousands of Russians from starving to death, including, no doubt, some Communists.

Sixteen years passed before President Roosevelt recognized the Soviet Union in 1933. Great Britain, France, and others had taken the step years earlier. Ironically, 1933 was also the year in which Adolf Hitler gained control of Germany, laying the groundwork for an even more horrendous round of war. Under Hitler, Germany began arming at a frightening pace while demanding "living space" for its people. For the Russians, the demands spelled fresh aggression and invasion. Once Hitler militarized the west bank of the Rhine River without opposition from France or Britain, the die seemed cast. Within the Soviet Union, Stalin stepped up the purges of his enemies real and imagined. Although he strengthened his personal control of party and state, he weakened the Soviet armed forces disastrously.

Meanwhile, the United States in the 1930s was still deep in its trance of isolationism that went back to George Washington's warning of "no entangling alliances." Americans believed that with two great oceans they were safe from foreign rivalries, unless they chose to become involved. Even in World War I, the United States was an Associated Power with Britain and France rather than a full-fledged Ally. Moreover, at the end of the war, despite President Wilson's efforts, the U.S. Senate refused to ratify the Treaty of Versailles or United States membership in the League of Nations. The alarms that rang in Europe and the Far East as Germany and Japan looked beyond their frontiers aroused some Americans, but they were in the smallest of minorities. The Great Depression had finally ended by the late 1930s, but the United States was still a country concerned with its problems at home.

The failure of Britain and France in 1938 to oppose Hitler's annexation of Austria and their agreement at Munich to his partition of Czechoslovakia convinced Stalin that he would have no ally against Germany, if Hitler looked his way. Better than anyone else, the Soviet dictator knew how weak his nation was. After all, he had ordered the deaths of many of the nation's best generals and leaders. His solution was a nonaggression treaty with Hitler in August 1939. Under the terms of the Molotov-Ribbentrop Pact, named for the foreign ministers of the two countries, Poland was partitioned. The deal returned to Russia part of its old Polish holdings and satisfied Hitler's need for a fresh conquest. On September 1, 1939, the Germans crossed into Poland. This time Britain and France reacted. On September 3, 1939, they declared war against Germany. World War II had begun.

The fighting moved so slowly at first that it was dubbed a "phony war." Suddenly, the Germans exploded northward through Norway and Denmark in April 1940, then westward in May through the Low Countries and into France. By June 14, 1940, the Germans were in Paris. Only the United Kingdom across the narrow English Channel opposed Germany in the west. But the British held. The Royal Air Force beat back the

German Luftwaffe and thwarted an invasion. Germany was stopped in the west. On June 22, 1941, the Germans swung east toward the Soviet Union. Stalin's fears of a German invasion had proved accurate.

The new German attack made Great Britain and the Soviet Union allies in the face of a common, deadly foe. But it did not make them friends. Russia's invasion of Poland on September 19, 1939 to claim its share of that helpless country, to be followed two and one-half months later by an unprovoked attack on small, democratic Finland were treacherous acts in the Western view. They were seen as examples of Soviet ruthlessness, if no nation was strong enough to stop it. The Soviets made no apologies. They said they had gained time and a buffer before an inevitable German attack. They argued that if the British and French had had the guts to stand fast with them in 1938 in opposing Hitler's grab of Czechoslovakia, World War II could have been avoided.

Between the start of war in Europe and V-E Day (Victory in Europe) nearly six years would elapse. From the Japanese attack on Pearl Harbor on December 7, 1941 and V-J Day (Victory in Japan) on August 15, 1945, nearly four years would pass. During that time, changes were set in motion that would crumble the empires of both losers and winners. New nations would be created and new power centers would emerge. The United States and the Union of Soviet Socialist Republics would become the undisputed Big Two of the postwar world—but as rivals, not as partners. In any event, the joining of the USSR, United States, and Britain in a common struggle was the result of circumstances rather than choice. Throughout the war, the United States and Britain were reluctant allies with the USSR.

[15]

Each side distrusted the other's form of government, style of life, political and military intentions and ambitions. Wartime propaganda and patriotic appeals to rally round the flag were not much help either. Each declared that it fought for victory and destruction of the Hitlerite foe on behalf of all people. Each proclaimed its brand of democracy to be the only genuine article.

The fundamental differences between the U.S.-U.K. and the USSR in their forms of government became more pointed once they started to win the war. As the Nazis were forced back from the captive lands of Western and Eastern Europe, those nations took their first steps toward reestablishing national governments. That meant East-West confrontation. The gap in 1945 and 1946 between what each meant by "free elections" finally proved unbridgeable in the case of Poland.

A Polish government-in-exile had been set up in Paris in 1939, then transferred to London in June 1940. Polish troops who had escaped the Germans fought on the Western fronts throughout World War II. An underground Home Army harassed the Germans from within. The exile government leaders expected that as soon as the Nazis had been expelled, they would take over an independent Poland. Stanislaw Mikolajczyk, who had become premier of the exiled government in 1943, enjoyed the backing of Churchill and Roosevelt and believed Stalin would accept his government as well. Instead, as the Red Army began to push the Nazis westward in the middle of 1944, Stalin turned over administration of the reconquered Polish lands to a group of Polish Communists. The Communists had been set up by the Russians in Lublin, a city southeast of Warsaw, as the Committee of National Liberation. The Lublin government now became a rival of the London exile government, with a crucial advantage. It was physically in Poland with the support of the Soviet Union. Mikolajczyk and his supporters were hundreds of miles distant. On August 1, 1944 as the Red Army neared Warsaw, thirty-five thousand poorly armed Poles of the Home Army, loyal to Mikolajczyk, attacked the powerful German garrison in the Polish capital. The Poles fought bravely, expecting help within days from the Russians. None came. American and British pleas to Stalin for assistance were rebuffed. After two months of desperate fighting, the Home Army was crushed. The Soviets liberated Warsaw in January 1945 and the Lublin Committee became the provisional Polish government. In the Big Three meetings at Yalta in February 1945 and at Potsdam in July 1945, the Americans and British accepted Soviet promises that there would be free elections in Poland. They consoled themselves that even though the provisional Communist government in Warsaw was an outrage, everything would be set right once the Poles voted. Those free elections were never held.

Poles in Britain and the United States and their many supporters felt betrayed. Roosevelt, in particular, was condemned for "selling out" Poland and other Eastern European countries at Yalta. Thereafter, the issue of free elections in Poland became the touchstone in the West for Soviet intentions.

It is clear that the seeds of the Cold War existed before the jostling began for liberated territories. That was a symptom rather than the cause of mutual hostility, according to some historians. But other historians have argued that the course of history after 1945 could have been altered, had the wartime Allies maintained their unity. The fact is that even during the fighting, the Soviet Union and the Western Allies were not drawn truly closer to each other in the ways that Americans and British were. In 1941, 1942, and 1943, as the Russians shouldered the brunt of the German assaults, they sought relief through the opening of a second front in the West. The Americans and British moving slowly through North Africa decided to seek their first foothold on the continent in Italy rather than trying a cross-Channel smash into France. Stalin, however, was convinced that political rather than military strategy dictated the U.S.-U.K. moves. Even after the Allies landed in Normandy and then in the south of France, the Russians insisted that Winston Churchill, with no strong disagreement from Roosevelt, was bent on letting Russia and Germany destroy each other before the United States and United Kingdom moved into a totally helpless Europe.

Soviet fears were not entirely fantasy. Churchill made no secret of his belief that political goals were at least as important as military ones. He pressed repeatedly for striking through the "soft underbelly" of the Balkans and capturing Berlin and Prague. To no avail. As the war drew to a close, accounts of secret negotiations in Switzerland and Italy by Western agents and German envoys spurred Soviet beliefs that even at the moment of victory, Nazi Germany might be turned eastward to wound the USSR further with its dying embrace. There never was a separate peace, but neither was there an end to Stalin's steadfast conviction that the West only awaited the proper moment to destroy his nation. Of this stuff was the Cold War, nurtured by decades of mutual threats, suspected double crosses, and genuine fear, brought to birth.

The Iron Curtain Descends

The dropping of the atomic bomb by the United States, first on Hiroshima, then on Nagasaki, at a stroke brought down the curtain on the hot war and raised it on the Cold War.

At Potsdam, the suburban town outside Berlin where the Big Three met in July 1945 to settle the occupation of Germany, President Truman received word of the first successful testing of a U.S. nuclear device in the New Mexico desert. The Americans at Potsdam were exultant, but uncertain whether and how much to reveal to the Russians. Truman finally told Stalin in a casual, almost offhand manner that the United States had developed a "new weapon of unusual destructive force." He did not say it was an A-bomb. In fact, Stalin knew from his spies what it was.

Without the A-bomb, American military planners said that it might cost one million U.S. casualties, perhaps half of them fatalities, to defeat Japan. Nevertheless, Secretary of War Henry Stimson argued against dropping the bomb on the Japanese city. Others proposed that the Japanese be given a demonstration of its lethal powers before destroying a large, densely populated area. We now know that the Japanese were prepared to negotiate a surrender before the bomb was dropped, although they insisted on retaining the emperor. Indeed, they tried to negotiate through the Soviets. Unfortunately for them, the Russians stalled in relaying the information to the United States. Instead, two days after the bombing of Hiroshima on August 6, 1945, the Soviets invaded Manchuria in keeping with an earlier agreement with the

United States. Later the Russians claimed that their entry into the war forced Japan's surrender, and that dropping the A-bomb was unnecessary. Japanese diehards who wanted to fight on even after the second bombing at Nagasaki reinforced the Americans who insisted that only the bomb brought the war to a dramatic end.

Whatever alternatives might have been available, President Truman's decision to use the bomb was keyed to ending the war. Over and beyond that reason, the United States also wished to demonstrate to the Soviets and to the rest of the world that America was the strongest military power on earth. Given its overwhelming atomic superiority, the United States was able to demobilize 90 percent of its armed forces and shift quickly to a peacetime economy that emphasized consumer goods at home and vigorous trade abroad. As for Stalin, he was right in regarding the A-bomb as a warning and a threat. But he showed no sign that he was frightened. To the contrary, he kept the Soviet armed forces at combat strength, using them to consolidate and police the territory over which the Soviets had sway.

To come back to Potsdam in July 1945, the purpose of the leaders of the United States, the Union of Soviet Socialist Republics, and the United Kingdom was to prepare a peace treaty with Germany and to settle the boundaries of postwar Europe. As it turned out, neither side intended to sign a peace treaty except on its own terms. The result was a division of Germany with the Soviets controlling roughly one-third the country, the United States, Britain, and France two-thirds. In addition, the Russians had sliced off the eastern provinces of Germany and placed them under Polish administration as consolation for having annexed Poland's eastern territories in 1939.

Of equal significance, the Big Three, as the United States, USSR, and United Kingdom were called, agreed, in effect, that each would have its "sphere of influence." For the USSR, this meant a decisive voice in Eastern Europe with Finland, Czechoslovakia, and Yugoslavia enjoying a more independent status. In Western Europe, the United States was the predominant power. Greece, the eastern Mediterranean, and the Middle East were recognized to be of special interest to the British.

To their people, Stalin and Truman made declarations of noble intent; neither would admit to the practice of "power politics" or interfering in the affairs of other nations. To that extent, both talked one way and acted another. Nevertheless, in the United States and the USSR the nature of each government moved its leaders to behave in widely contrasting manner. An American president is rarely a robot, responding automatically to "the will of the people." But he dare not ignore the electorate if he wishes to get his legislation passed. In 1945 and 1946, the American voters wanted cars, homes, and appliances, not large standing armies. Furthermore, Truman had to walk a careful line between rows of critics. Thus, former Vice-President Henry Wallace attacked Truman for being too warlike with the Russians and threatening the peace, and Senators Mundt, Jenner, and Knowland denounced him for being soft on Communism. Also, while the United States had the power and money to influence governments in devastated Western Europe, powerful Communist parties in France and Italy shouted and waved their fists at the "ugly Americans."

In the Soviet Union, on the other hand, whatever dissent existed within the ruling Politburo or on the part of the people was not made public. The scale of Stalin's purges in the 1930s was not repeated. But from 1945 onward, millions of citizens were arrested for political reasons, including tens of thousands who had been German prisoners of war and therefore were regarded as "unreliable." Consumer demand was ignored. In the USSR, there were no politicians running on a "bring the boys back home" platform, since there were no opposition parties. In Eastern European countries, such as Hungary and Bulgaria, the opposition that existed was short-lived.

It has been said that at the end of the Potsdam Conference, Truman, Stalin, and Clement Attlee, who had succeeded Churchill as the British prime minister, did not write a peace treaty as expected. Rather, they signed what amounted to a tripartite declaration of the Cold War. That may be a melodramatic reading of what happened. Nevertheless, if neither the United States nor the USSR actively sought the Cold War, each seemed quick enough to accept it. Averell Harriman, the U.S. ambassador to Moscow and personally close to Stalin, advised Presidents Roosevelt and Truman that the Soviets had legitimate interests which must be respected, but that what the Russians understood most clearly was strength. In the face of weakness, they would push, push, push until they found an opening through which they could pour. Harriman had cabled Truman while the argument about free elections in Poland raged back and forth. "I am afraid Stalin does not and never will fully understand our interest in a free Poland as a matter of principle. He is a realist in all of his actions, and it is hard for him to appreciate our faith in abstract principles. It is difficult for him to understand why we should want to interfere with Soviet policy in a country like Poland, which he considers so important to

Russia's security, unless we have some ulterior motive." Of course, the influence of Americans of Polish descent in an election was not a factor fully acknowledged.

Although Yalta and Potsdam recognized that there would be spheres of influence, there were also gray areas on the world map. One such area was Iran. Iran has a common border with the USSR, but was led by an anti-Communist shah. The United States, United Kingdom, and USSR had agreed to withdraw their troops from that country at war's end, but first the Soviets wanted to extract oil concessions. In February and March 1946, the Soviets sent tanks toward the Iranian frontier to emphasize her wishes. Secretary of State James Byrnes warned the Russians to withdraw. The Soviets stalled, then at the beginning of May ordered the Red Army out of Iran. About the same time, the Soviets tried to pressure another country next to them, Turkey, into granting joint control of the strategic Dardanelles Strait, which provides passage from the Black Sea to the Mediterranean. The United States dispatched a naval unit toward the strait and the Soviets eased off.

On the other hand, in Poland and in other countries bordering their frontiers in Eastern Europe, the Russians rejected all outside interference or protest. The Communist governments in those countries carried out orders from Moscow without question.

A real arena for struggle in the Cold War was Greece, where the Communist party was strong but not overpowering. Great Britain had been assigned a major role in that country, but by 1946 Britain's economy was too weak to support the full weight of its international military and economic commitments. At U.S. insistence, an international commission had supervised

the Greek elections of March 1946. King George's pro-Western party won, whereupon the Greek Communists, supported by Bulgaria and Yugoslavia, started a civil war. With the British too hard pressed to shore up their Greek allies, the United States agreed to step in. But a problem quickly developed. Isolationism in the United States was far from dead, and at the beginning of 1947 a newly elected budget-cutting Republican Congress was opposed to pouring money into foreign countries. To get Congress to change its mind, President Truman turned for help to a leading Republican senator, Arthur Vandenberg. Together, they warned that *both* military and economic aid were necessary in order to stem the tide of Communism. In what became known as the Truman Doctrine, the president declared in March 1947 that "totalitarian regimes imposed on free peoples by direct or indirect aggression" were a threat to general peace. That was enough to swing congressional votes in his direction for aid to Greece and to Turkey.

The division between a Free World and a Communist World had been dramatized nearly a year earlier by Winston Churchill. In a speech at Fulton, Missouri, on March 5, 1946, Churchill declared: "From Stettin in the Baltic to Trieste in the Adriatic an iron curtain has descended across the continent."

The image of Communist troops overwhelming Europe,

Greece was an early area of struggle in the Cold War after World War II. Here two groups of guerrillas pose during 1947.

[25]

then breaking out into the Middle East, Africa, and Asia may have been the most important influence in persuading reluctant congressmen to approve aid to Greece and Turkey. But the leaders of Western Europe saw the greater danger to their way of life in 1946–47 coming from economic collapse rather than military invasion. The recognition of this economic danger led U.S. Secretary of State George C. Marshall to make an historic speech at Harvard in June 1947. He called for massive economic assistance that would put Europe back on its feet. It was promptly called the Marshall Plan rather than by its official designation, the Organization for European Economic Cooperation. Initially, membership was extended to the Soviet Union and the nations of Eastern as well as Western Europe. The USSR attended an organizing meeting in Paris but declined to join. Poland and Czechoslovakia indicated they would, but the Russians said *nyet*, and they withdrew.

More than $12 billion ($12,000,000,000) of U.S. aid was pumped into Western Europe through the Marshall Plan, and it paid off. Revitalized nations regained their footing and started the march toward a more unified alliance than had ever existed in Europe under peaceful conditions. Not by accident, a reborn Western Europe was a major customer for U.S. exports as those countries again developed the means to produce goods, earn foreign exchange, and trade in international markets.

Along with economic rebuilding came a military alliance in 1949 known as the North Atlantic Treaty Organization (NATO). The United States was the chief supplier of troops and armaments including its awesome atomic power. But the treaty required each member—there were twelve originally—to contribute armed forces to defend the whole organization. The European nations were shrewd enough to take advantage of U.S. fears of a Communist-dominated Europe to leave the chief burden to the United States. But as time went by and their economic conditions improved, they found that they had a greater stake in protecting what they had.

Through the years, the Cold War and the Iron Curtain always were most clearly in evidence in Germany. At war's end, the Russians had demanded $20 billion ($20,000,000,000) in reparations for the Allies from Germany. The Western powers never agreed to a figure, and before too many months shut off reparations from their zones, leaving the Russians to strip what they could from the Soviet zone. Compared with what was going on in the Soviet zone, the Western zones received generous treatment, and in time began to show it. West Germany's economic recovery triggered angry denunciations from the Russians that the United States, United Kingdom, and France were intent on reviving a warlike Germany. As competition between the United States and the USSR became more intense, the two parts of Germany were pulled farther apart, despite the wishes of Germans themselves for reunification.

A confrontation was not long in coming. When the Western powers reformed West Germany's currency, the D-mark, the Russians imposed a partial blockade on Berlin. More than 100 miles (161 kilometers) inside the Soviet zone, West Berlin had been a thorn in the side of the USSR and the East German Communists. By taking an underground train or streetcar, East Berliners could cross into West Berlin and see the contrast in life-styles under Western flags. Many who crossed did not return.

East Germans in increasing numbers were using Berlin as an escape hatch to the West. Sure enough, when the Western powers announced their intention of allowing a new German D-mark to circulate in Berlin, the Soviets made their blockade complete in June 1948.

Communist theory scoffed at the ability of capitalist nations to reform themselves and improve their conditions. But in practice, the Soviet leaders understood quickly enough that a new currency in West Germany would help that country's economy. They knew too that a new D-mark circulating in West Berlin would make the East German mark look bad in comparison. It was a comparison they were determined to avoid.

The Soviet blockade cut off all supplies going to West Berlin by road, rail, and waterway. The Soviets expected West Berlin and the Western Allies to cave in, and then they could take over the entire city. Instead, the Americans and British put together an airlift. The "air bridge" as the Germans called it, kept enough food and coal flowing into West Berlin to allow two million inhabitants to survive the winter.

Before the airlift had proved itself, the U.S. commander in Germany, General Lucius Clay, talked of an armed train forcing a passage across East Germany with troops and tanks moving along the Autobahn. The shadow of war deterred the U.S. Joint Chiefs of Staff from endorsing the plan. But the airlift worked. Neither side was put to the final test of will. In May 1949, the Russians quietly informed the Americans at the United Nations that they were ready to lift the blockade.

Determination, ingenuity, and courage had worked for the Americans and British. The lives lost in the airlift seemed worth

German workers unload a U.S. "Flying Box-
car" plane, a workhorse of the U.S. airlift to
Berlin during 1948–1949. Each plane carried
nearly eight tons of heavy goods and equipment.

the price of maintaining the Western foothold behind the Iron Curtain. Beyond that, the countries of Western Europe drew more closely together. Moved by the grit of the West Berliners and the willingness of the United States, United Kingdom, and France to stand by their commitments, they ratified the NATO agreement in April 1949, even as the Soviets prepared to lift the blockade.

Meanwhile, the three western zones of Germany had gained in respectability. Carrying the name the Federal Republic of Germany, the three zones had taken a long step from a defeated enemy to a tentative ally. True, the Soviets had made their countermoves between 1947 and 1949. They had formed an economic alliance called Comecon; a military alliance called the Warsaw Pact; and a political organization, the Cominform. Determined to be first with something, the Soviets announced the creation in East Germany of the German Democratic Republic before the announcement of the formation of the Federal Republic in West Germany. Each side had learned that in the Cold War, as in a hot war, the threat from the other side is a powerful unifier. In the future, the menace of the other, actual or potential, was a potent weapon in putting down dissent at home or among one's allies.

The Western victory in Berlin brought a brief hope that the Soviets had been taught a lesson and would hesitate to use their muscle elsewhere. But the balance of power was about to be tipped ominously. In September 1949—barely four years after the United States had dropped the first atomic bomb—the Soviet Union exploded an A-bomb of its own. It was a stunning development.

The Cold War at Home

To many Americans, it was inconceivable that the Russians could have developed an atomic bomb on their own. Even with the forced help of captured German scientists and engineers, the Soviets simply were not credited with the know-how needed to put together a superweapon, as the United States had. Consequently, if the Russians really had an A-bomb—and many Americans doubted that they did—there was only one explanation: the Soviets had been given vital top-secret American information. They had received the information either through a spy network or been handed it by American traitors in high office.

A real puzzle, nevertheless, was how the Soviet Union had managed to do the job if it had required help from within. The Communist party in the United States has always been tiny. Its candidates for president have never received more than a relative handful of votes. No person has ever won election to the U.S. Congress running on the Communist party ticket. It had no allies in the major parties.

In such a setting, how could American citizens who were Communists or who were sympathetic to Communism and the Soviet Union (they were dubbed "fellow travelers") threaten the security of the United States? The debate on that subject provoked the country as have few issues in recent times. As the Cold War escalated in intensity, debate turned into a near life-and-death struggle. At stake was the right to work, and even to stay out of jail, for those in television, radio, journalism, motion pictures, drama, literature, the law, and government who would not cooperate with congressional investigating committees.

An early storm was created by Henry A. Wallace. Wallace had been vice-president in the third administration of Franklin Roosevelt. But he was passed over for renomination in 1944 and therefore denied the presidency when Roosevelt died early in his fourth term. As secretary of commerce in President Truman's cabinet, Wallace argued for friendship and cooperation with the Soviet Union. As Truman and his secretary of state, James Byrnes, became tougher in dealing with the Russians, Wallace spoke out more loudly in opposition. In the fall of 1946, Truman fired him. Wallace retaliated by running for president in 1948 on a newly formed Progressive party ticket that had obvious Communist support. Wallace hoped to draw enough liberal support away from Truman to defeat him, but Truman won.

Wallace was called "soft on Communism," "appeaser," and many other things. But so were other politicians at that time including Dean Acheson, who became Truman's secretary of state in 1949. Later, in the 1960s and 1970s, Acheson was described as a "cold warrior" because of his anti-Soviet positions. But the mood of the immediate postwar years was such that defending someone charged with Communist sympathies was taken as a sign of being "pinko," "ultraliberal," or a "Communist sympathizer." Scant attention was paid to the actual views or records of those charged.

Dean Acheson became a particular target of the anti-Communists because of his testimony for a friend and colleague in the State Department, Alger Hiss. Hiss had been a prominent career State Department official who helped write the United Nations charter, and had accompanied President Roosevelt to Yalta in February 1945. To some, the United Nations from its outset was regarded as a haven for Communist nations and anyone involved with it was automatically suspect. In congressional hearings that brought him national attention, a young congressman, Richard M. Nixon, accused Hiss of having passed secrets to the Communists in the 1930s. Hiss denied the charge, but was found guilty in January 1950 of lying under oath (perjury). Acheson refused to denounce Hiss, saying he would not turn his back on his colleague.

Acheson's refusal was like trailing blood before a shark, as far as the anti-Communists were concerned. No wonder the United States had not won the Cold War, they declared, when the enemy had agents in high places. In an effort to defuse the criticism, President Truman appointed a Loyalty Review Board. Its job was to make sure that there were no subversives or unreliable persons in government who might betray official secrets. But there was no foolproof way of proving one's loyalty, short of joining the ranks of the Communist-hunters. The history of purges in other countries was a frightening signal to liberty-minded Americans.

The man who came to symbolize the witch-hunt against Communists was U.S. Senator Joseph McCarthy. A Republican from Wisconsin, McCarthy burst upon the national consciousness in February 1950 with a charge that he had a list of 205 Communists employed by the State Department. Only days before, Klaus Fuchs, a British atomic scientist who had worked at Los Alamos on the U.S. A-bomb project, was arrested as a member of a Soviet spy ring. It was an ideal springboard for McCarthy. In the time that followed, the number of McCarthy's alleged Communists in the State Department changed from 205 to 57 to 81. The targets changed from civilians in high government office to Army officers to other senators. "Proof" was never produced. But the fears that McCarthy raised and his power to intimidate grew by leaps and bounds. So powerful did McCarthy consider himself that in 1952 he attacked General Marshall, then secretary of defense, as part of a "conspiracy so immense and an infamy so black as to dwarf any previous such venture in the history of man." McCarthy was able to bully General Dwight Eisenhower, who owed his meteoric military rise to Marshall, to the extent that Eisenhower, running for president, failed to defend his old chief publicly or to denounce McCarthy.

The Democrats scurried furiously to disprove accusations that poured like rain from the skies. The Truman Loyalty Boards screened nearly 5 million federal employees and dismissed only 560 on "grounds relating to loyalty"—not the same, by any means, as proving them Communists or spies. To no avail. After Eisenhower was elected president, the Republicans rescreened all federal employees but found fewer than 500 additional cases involving "subversives."

While McCarthy and the Loyalty Boards scoured the ranks of government repeatedly, the House Committee on Un-American Activities turned its spotlight on writers, television performers, Hollywood actors and directors, college professors, lawyers, labor leaders, and an assortment of others. The pressure to turn informer, to make public confession, to name others, and to join the army of rooters-out-of-Communism was intense. That there were genuine, certified spies at work was not the issue. Espionage is the practice of all governments; the larger and more powerful the nation the more sophisticated its intelligence activities and "dirty tricks" departments. What was noteworthy in the United States during this period was the hysteria that a charge of Communism could arouse, regardless of how flimsy the evidence. The notion that if there was no wrongdoing, there was nothing to fear or hide was disproved by Senator McCarthy's smears against decorated war heroes and even against General Marshall—a man who was wartime Army chief of staff, U.S. secretary of state, and secretary of defense.

Why were Democratic and Republican presidents so helpless in dealing with McCarthy? To begin with, in order to convince Congress that the Cold War had to be supported unsparingly, they painted the Communists in the blackest terms. If the menace of Soviet aggression and conspiracy was so serious as to require billions of dollars for nations abroad, how could a president shrug at anyone in the United States who was less than 100 percent loyal? In short, since economic aid was tied to military aid in order to win the Cold War, the Cold War abroad meant a united anti-Communist front at home.

Of course, there were strong supporters of constitutional rights, presumption of innocence until proved guilty, and trial by jury rather than by congressional committee. But it was a tough, uphill battle. And inevitably something would happen at home or abroad that allowed the superpatriots to paint themselves as the only reliable defenders of the Republic.

The amazing achievement of the Russians in exploding an A-bomb in 1949, years before the United States thought them capable of the feat; the arrest of Klaus Fuchs; and other spy disclosures in the United States, Canada, and Britain set the stage for an event that still haunts some Americans. In 1950, a

Assistant Defense Secretary H. Struve Hensel (left) glares at McCarthy (right) during the McCarthy-Army dispute in April 1954.

husband and wife, Julius and Ethel Rosenberg, both native-born Americans, were arrested and charged with having passed nuclear weapons secrets to the Soviets. The chief prosecution witness was Mrs. Rosenberg's brother, David Greenglass, also accused of being part of the plot. The Rosenbergs claimed their innocence to the end, but they were convicted of espionage. Despite worldwide protests, they were electrocuted in June 1953. The Rosenbergs' sons, now grown, have reopened the case and, using FBI files, have raised questions about documents that helped convict their parents.

McCarthy finally met his Waterloo in the United States Senate. It started with a Senate committee sitting between April and June 1954 to decide on charges that the Department of the Army and Senator McCarthy leveled against each other. It led to McCarthy becoming ever more reckless in his denunciations and abuse of fellow senators. It ended with McCarthy tried and censured by the full Senate of the United States in January 1955. From that point on, the force of the McCarthy anti-Communist campaign was spent. By then, the tides had changed in the Soviet Union as well.

During the height of the McCarthy era in the United States, the Soviet Union was in the thrall of Josef Stalin's last fit of madness in which he saw the entire world conspiring against him. His accusations and purges had reached a point where his oldest and closest colleagues, who had survived more than forty years alongside him, feared that they too might be killed. Stalin raised again the hobgoblin of "capitalist encirclement" bent on destroying the USSR. Within the Soviet Union, the work camps and political prisons were packed. With his finger within reach of the A-bomb button, Stalin's associates hesitated no longer. In what is generally considered to have been the highest-level decision of the ranking Politburo members, Stalin's security chief in the Kremlin was announced dead one day in February 1953. Three weeks later, Stalin was dead. Officially, it was termed a "hemorrhage of the brain."

Although the United States and the Soviet Union are drastically different in the form and operation of government, both used the threat of destruction from the other to carry forward its policies. In the Soviet Union, Stalin consistently spurned more consumer goods, lighter controls of the lives of the people, and less repression toward the satellite countries. He justified his actions on the basis that to do otherwise would play into the hands of capitalist spies and enemies at home and abroad. Only after Stalin passed from the scene did the USSR seek to make changes both in domestic policies and in its relations with the West.

In the United States, humanitarian reasons probably would not have been sufficient to convince Congress to provide huge amounts of economic aid to Western Europe, Japan, and other countries in Asia, Africa, and Latin America. But by making economic assistance and then military aid to pro-U.S. governments part of the war against Communism—the Cold War—the Democrats were able to win over Congress. The price of conformity, of toeing the line, was not in any way comparable in the United States with the USSR. At the height of McCarthyism, courageous men and women spoke out, disregarding personal risk. Senators Wayne Morse and Margaret Chase Smith took the floor of the Senate to denounce McCarthy early in the Wisconsinite's career. And on radio and television, Elmer Davis and Edward R. Murrow led a fight against fear, insisting that one could be a loyal American and a critic of McCarthy at the same time. Others less well known lost their jobs, friends, and reputations for speaking out. But they were not sent to prison camps, tortured, or killed. Nevertheless, by American standards, the modern witch-hunt was a low point with regard to protection of individual rights and liberties.

As we look back, we can recognize that the Soviets used spies, both native and foreign, in order to gather information. All large countries do. They also go to great lengths to block their opponents from doing likewise by "counterintelligence" or "state security." Ordinary citizens may dislike espionage of any kind and feel it should be abolished, but it is a fact of life.

The Russians were able to subvert citizens of the United States, Great Britain, and Canada to work for them through a combination of ideology, bribery, and blackmail. But skilled Soviet agents were presumably much more important in stealing important secrets. And the congressional investigating committees, loyalty boards, and private "Red-hunting" agencies that gained so much publicity did little to thwart those spies. Counterintelligence belongs to the professionals. In the United States, that responsibility belongs to the Federal Bureau of Investigation (FBI) domestically, and to the Central Intelligence Agency (CIA), National Security Agency (NSA), and other agencies involved with U.S. foreign affairs. The chiefs of the FBI and of the CIA, as discovered during the Watergate investigations, have sometimes broken the law and tried to justify their actions because of "national security." Most Americans reject their law-breaking, and support steps to prevent its happening again. Nevertheless, a government cannot safely abolish its security agencies, and therefore does not.

America and Its Allies

Until not too long ago, Americans thought of themselves as members of a young nation, still close in spirit to the days of their own revolution. They found a natural sympathy with the notion that colonial countries would and should free themselves of their rulers. Wise rulers, they pointed out, voluntarily surrendered power as their colonies became able to govern themselves, and thereby won their friendship. As an example, the United States pointed with self-satisfaction to its grant of independence to the Philippines in 1946.

The first American president, George Washington, had warned in his farewell address against "entangling alliances." His successors found it good advice. Together with the Monroe Doctrine it provided the United States with the basis for being top dog in the Western Hemisphere and getting involved only occasionally elsewhere. In the nineteenth century, the small Army, Navy, and Marine Corps were big enough to punish the Barbary pirates in the Mediterranean, force Japan to make trade concessions, and to push Spain out of Cuba and the Philippines.

Of course, as a growing world power, the United States sometimes found it necessary to make common cause with other great powers. The most striking case was during World War I when the United States joined Britain and France "to make the world safe for democracy." Above all, the United States saw itself as free, fair, generous, a haven to the oppressed, the champion of the underdog.

In the 1930s, the economically profitable military interventions in Latin America gave way to a "Good Neighbor" policy under President Franklin D. Roosevelt. Trade and friendship rather than the Marines were to be the means of cementing the ties between the United States and Latin America. During World War II, Latin American nations were well represented among the victorious Allies. After the war, many of them were charter members of the United Nations. On the surface, the Good Neighbor policy seemed to work.

As for the country to the north, Americans viewed the great lands of Canada, larger in size than the United States, as an unexplored frontier thinly populated with friendly Canadians and Eskimos. Canada was a dominion of Great Britain before World War II, but with its open border and common language, Canadians were regarded as almost-Americans. Only an accident, it might be argued, had prevented Canada from formally becoming part of the Union, and now it hardly mattered. In World Wars I and II, Canadians had fought with distinction and bravery at the side of the British. Americans impatient to join the battle prior to U.S. entry into the wars had enlisted in the Canadian armed forces. The United States might have a Good Neighbor policy toward Latin America, but Canada *was* the good neighbor. Its leaders were as respected in Washington as they were in London.

In the United Nations, Canada and the Latin American countries tended to vote solidly with the United States throughout the 1950s and into the 1960s. It gave the United States a handy majority in the General Assembly where each nation had one vote. In the Security Council where the major powers, the United States, USSR, United Kingdom, France, and China, had accepted a rule of unanimity, Soviet vetoes could be branded as evidence that the Russians were indifferent to the will of the majority. The "will of the majority" in the General Assembly would haunt and mock the United States in the late 1960s and 1970s, but that was still a long way in the future. In the meantime, the almost automatic backing of the Americas led the United States to take the support of those countries very much for granted as the Cold War intensified.

The governments of the Western Hemisphere, by and large, found it in their own interests to side with the United States against the Russians, and to oppose admission of the Chinese Communists to the U.N. The majority of countries to the south of Mexico were run by military leaders. The prospect of Communism taking hold was no more to their liking than it was to the United States'. In 1954 when a rightist group, backed by the United States, overthrew the Communist-supported government of Colonel Arbenz in Guatemala, the other right-wing Latin American governments were not greatly disturbed.

During the mid and late 1950s, however, discontent, unrest, and upheaval shook the seats of military right-wing dictators in various Latin American countries. Drastic cutbacks in economic aid by the Eisenhower administration during those years added to both governmental and popular resentment of the United States. Within the Organization of American States, grumbles about the United States grew louder. And public sentiment was so strongly anti-*Yanqui* in parts of Latin America that Vice-President Nixon was pelted with eggs in the streets of Peru and Venezuela when he toured in 1958. Thus, the stage was set for Fidel Castro to overthrow the dictator Batista in Cuba in 1959 and set up a socialist-minded government.

*A Venezuelan woman shouts into the car
carrying Vice-President Nixon during a tour
of Caracas in 1959. Angry crowds threw
rocks and hit the car with heavy sticks.*

What set Castro apart from other Latin rebels, however, was his refusal to pay U.S. companies in hard cash for lands and properties that he nationalized. Instead, he offered long-term notes. From that point on, U.S.-Cuban relations went from bad to worse. To gain leverage against the United States, Castro accepted Soviet economic and military aid including advisers. After the U.S.-supported invasion of Cuba in April 1961 at the Bay of Pigs failed, Castro went even further. He agreed to allow the Soviets to install missiles on Cuban soil. Until then, Castro probably had most Latin Americans behind him, even if their governments felt obliged to back the United States publicly. But the vision of an advanced Soviet military base in the Western Hemisphere did not please the Latins very much. As for the United States, it was intolerable to have Soviet rockets ninety miles (145 kilometers) off the mainland, ready to strike.

The events of 1961 and 1962 revealed two important points about the Cold War. First, the United States no longer had "satellites" that would do its bidding; Castro had more popular support than the exiles. Second, the Cuban Missile Crisis in October 1962 demonstrated that the United States was ready to use its power when its direct national interest was at stake. Put to the test by the Soviets, the United States signaled its readiness to go to war unless the missiles were removed, and the Russians pulled out.

Efforts to establish a positive relationship between the United States and the Latin Americas, not based on the Cold War, have been more elusive. When John F. Kennedy became president, he proclaimed an "Alliance for Progress." He pledged $20 billion ($20,000,000,000) during the next decade for the general social and economic uplifting of the southern portion of the hemisphere. Latin Americans responded with hope to the promise of a more equal relationship. But President Kennedy was assassinated and with him died many of the expectations. In their stead came an angrier Latin view of the unequal seesaw that tilted heavily toward the north. The displeasure was reflected in a changing Latin view of the Cold War.

During the Korean War years of 1950–53, the Latin American nations stood by the United States and provided various forms of assistance including military units. During the Vietnam War, especially during the years of deepest U.S. involvement in the middle and late 1960s, there was no such common interest. Nor was the United States able to maintain a solid front among the Latin Americans against the admission to the U.N. of the People's Republic of China. Within the Organization of American States, the United States was a reluctant follower when that body voted to readmit Cuba to membership. During the terms of Presidents Johnson, Nixon, and Ford there were periods of renewed attention to the southern nations. But the effect of the Cold War was to cause first neglect by the United States, then hostile divisions between South and North America, and finally greater identification by the Latin nations with the Third World of Africa and Asia.

Canada suffered, as did Latin America, from the overwhelming industrial, technological, and financial strength of the United States. Wholly owned subsidiaries of big American firms based in Canada were considered by their top U.S. executives as branches of the parent, not as Canadian companies. A recession in the United States meant a recession in Canada. As the Canadians put it more sourly, "When the U.S. economy catches cold, the Canadians get pneumonia." Militarily the two were joined in the North American Air Defense Command, since together they were a major target for long-range Soviet bombers and missiles. In addition, Canada's close association with the United States and United Kingdom in World War II had given it special access to atomic secrets. That made Canada an important back door for the Soviet Union. The Russians established a major spy network in Canada that helped funnel atomic information to Moscow.

Nevertheless, Canada welcomed its role as a respected medium-sized power. A stout backer of the North Atlantic Treaty Organization (NATO) from its launching in 1949, Canada also played peacemaking roles in Indochina, the Sinai, Lebanon, and the Congo. Above all, it was successful in not being regarded as a satellite in the Cold War.

Wherever else skirmishes, encounters, and even major engagements occurred, the main stage of the Cold War continued to be in Europe. The countries of Western Europe were always mindful that the front lines of the Cold War were where they were. In the early postwar years, an exhausted Great Britain, faced with domestic economic troubles and a shrinking empire, welcomed U.S. willingness to shoulder Britain's former commitments in the world. But after decades of being on top, it was difficult to accept the United States as being number one. Ever sensitive to not being fully consulted or having its advice ignored, the British took to criticizing the American style of politics and diplomacy, calling it too naïve or too blunt, too slow to react or too hysterical. Of more substance was the British realization that the U.S. Congress, in throwing up high walls around nuclear secrets, was locking Great Britain out in the process. The result was a British decision to develop its own

A-bomb, in order to join a club to which the admission price was a nuclear bomb of one's own.

The French, feeling their reputation stained by the surrender to Germany in 1940 and by their poor-relative status among the Big Four, were in an even more difficult position. With a strong and noisy French Communist party plus a shaky economy, they were bedeviled by fears of the Red Army surging westward or of a reborn and rearmed Germany trying again to dominate central Europe. But General Charles de Gaulle, symbol of French wartime resistance and national self-esteem, had withdrawn from politics in 1946 and until his return as president in 1959, France followed an uncertain course.

The greatest impact of the Cold War on Western Europe, as we have noted, was in opening the U.S. Treasury for massive doses of economic aid through the Marshall Plan and of military aid through NATO. In combination, they allowed President Truman to convince the Congress and the American people that the best defensive lines against the Soviet Union and Communism should be drawn in Europe through Germany.

For Germany, the Cold War meant the loss for at least a generation and perhaps indefinitely of the dream of a reunified Reich. The Soviet Union and the United States both insisted they wanted reunification, but on terms unacceptable to the other. Nevertheless, some say that between the end of World War II and the building of the Berlin Wall in 1961 that sealed East Berlin off from West Berlin, there could have been a compromise that would have reunified *and* neutralized a new Germany. But neither side was willing to risk losing what it had.

For West Germany, in any case, the Cold War was a mixed blessing. It sped the Federal Republic of Germany (its official name) from despised and defeated enemy into a valued and sought-after ally. In fewer years than the wartime Allied chiefs would have predicted, German soldiers (both East and West) were carrying guns and drilling, with German leaders in the comfortable position of avoiding atomic armaments as unnecessary. In the face of a steadily reviving West Germany, Britain, France, Italy, and the Benelux nations (Belgium, the Netherlands, and Luxembourg) realized that they must take steps to keep the new republic inside the ring, not outside. The result of drawing West Germany closer was to tie Western Europe itself together more snugly economically, militarily, and politically. The signing of the European Economic Community (EEC) treaty on January 1, 1957 by six countries of Western Europe was the beginning of a new chapter of cooperation. It might have happened without the Cold War since the EEC helped the economies of its members. But the Cold War certainly helped speed it past rivalries and suspicions by drawing them together against a common foe.

Japan's defeat in World War II was even more total and shattering than Germany's. The use of two atomic bombs to obliterate Hiroshima and Nagasaki demonstrated the unquestioned military superiority of the Americans to the Japanese. And the installation of General of the Army Douglas MacArthur above the semidivine Emperor Hirohito was a political and spiritual conquest that was unsparing in its decisiveness. For a people to whom pride, self-respect, and "face" were so important, the humiliation was overwhelming. One result was a genuine unwillingness by the Japanese to rearm, even when in later years the United States pressed them to do so. In the early postwar years, however, the absence of the Russians on the main Japanese islands shielded Japan from the direct effects of the Cold War. But the coming defeat of the Nationalists on the Chinese mainland in 1949 soon convinced U.S. planners that Japan must become a "bulwark of democracy" in the East. That view plus the cooperative attitude of Emperor Hirohito toward the American occupiers loosened the U.S. purse strings. Japanese industry and the economy spurted. By 1950, the outbreak of the Korean War gave the Japanese a strong forward push and Washington and Tokyo began peace talks. In September 1951, a Japanese peace treaty was signed, with forty-eight nations on hand, in San Francisco. The Cold War was so intense at this stage that the peace treaty caused little agitation—all less than ten years from the bombing of Pearl Harbor, a day that President Roosevelt had predicted solemnly would "live in infamy."

The Cold War
Turns Hot: Korea

Under the rules of the Cold War, each side could manipulate, probe, and even skirmish provided it did not lead to a full-scale assault. In 1946–47, the United States and USSR had poked and parried at each other in Iran, Turkey, and Greece with tanks and warships. In Berlin, American GIs and Soviet Ivans had jostled each other at close quarters and trained tanks and cannons at the other.

Given the stakes and the delicate balance, no-war, no-peace could be murder on the nerves. The two nuclear superpowers have been described as two scorpions in a bottle. Each can kill the other, but in the act ensures its own death as well. In the early 1950s, the term *first-strike capability* was coined. Could either side, in attacking first, make sure that it had also destroyed the capability of the other to retaliate? Or could either withstand an initial attack and strike back with lethal force?

A more immediate problem for the United States was how to respond to limited aggression. What could the United States do, for example, if the Russians sliced off a chunk of Turkey or of West Germany? In the 1950s, with far fewer Americans than Russians under arms, and with the Western Europeans only slowly building up their armies, the United States could not match the enemy on the ground. The threat of dropping an A-bomb on Moscow or on Leningrad to hold the Russians in line was not convincing either. It could mean having a Soviet bomb dropped on Washington or on New York. To get through this impasse, American political and military planners devised a series of plans that involved a mixture of shield forces and tactical nuclear weapons in Europe. The shield was designed to put a screen of American soldiers in the way of Russian ground troops. Even if they could not contain the Soviets, U.S. troops would serve as a tripwire. Thereafter, tactical nuclear weapons could give the United States an effective counterpunch short of all-out war. This in a nutshell was the strategy of NATO for deterring the Russians, or if necessary of holding them to a standoff.

In fact, the United States' plans and practice campaigns failed to prepare the country for what would actually happen: a major war in a distant, scarcely known country called Korea. Whether the Korean War—the United States called it a "police action"—could have been avoided, or whether once started it could have ended in a clear-cut American victory has been argued for a quarter of a century. There is no agreement. Two points appear clear. The Communist-run government of North Korea, at the direction of the Soviet Union, acted on the assumption that the pro-U.S. South Koreans would collapse with a strong shove. Second, Secretary of State Acheson in a speech early in 1950 had placed Korea outside the U.S. zone of vital security in the Far East. The Soviets and North Koreans interpreted the speech to mean the United States would not get involved in a fight. They could find examples of America keeping hands off when the Communists seized power in Eastern Europe immediately after World War II and in 1948 when the Soviets forced a socialist but democratic Czech government to give way. It seemed a good risk.

On June 25, 1950, North Korean troops moving behind

Soviet-built tanks crossed the Thirty-eighth Parallel that divided the country and drove back the armies of South Korea. But the South Koreans did not surrender and the United States did not look the other way. President Truman ordered the U.S. Seventh Fleet to screen Formosa and dispatched military supplies to South Korea. Not sure what the real target of the attack was, Truman asked the Soviets, behind the scenes, to use their influence to pull the North Koreans back. Stalin refused. The U.N. Security Council, with the Soviets absent, passed a resolution 9–0 declaring the North Koreans aggressors and demanding their withdrawal. Within a week of the attack, U.S. troops were in South Korea, to be joined later by troops of other nations under an overall United Nations command.

Korea kept American servicemen fighting for three years in a war that seesawed back and forth. After being driven into a small pocket on the southeast coast of Korea, the U.N. forces in a brilliant end run landed behind the North Korean armies' lines and reversed the tide of battle. With the lure of a great victory before him, General MacArthur pushed his troops past the Thirty-eighth Parallel toward the Yalu River. Despite warnings that moving up to China's frontier would bring the Chinese into the war, MacArthur persisted. He had convinced civilian and military leaders in Washington that the war could be ended by Christmas 1950. The prediction was dead wrong. Hundreds of thousands of Chinese troops, calling themselves volunteers, poured across the Yalu, slicing into the thinly spread U.N. armies. As the fortunes of war turned toward the Communists, MacArthur demanded permission to bomb Chinese bases in Manchuria. Truman vetoed the proposal. He figured that bombing China would force the USSR to join the war openly on the side of the People's Republic of China.

U.N. troops advancing against Chinese Communist forces near Seoul, Korea.

Truman's refusal to expand the field of combat may have headed off World War III. It led to his dramatic firing of MacArthur in 1951. It also fueled the anti-Communists in the United States, who accused the president of a "no-win" policy. The election in 1952 of Dwight D. Eisenhower to succeed Truman finally opened the way to an armistice in Korea the following year. As a general, a war hero, and a Republican, Eisenhower was able to negotiate an armistice that could have been unacceptable coming from Democrat Harry Truman.

In that same year of 1953, after more than twenty-five years of despotic rule, a more moderate man, Georgi Malenkov, sat in Stalin's seat in the Kremlin. Malenkov tried to relax international tensions and to establish better relations with the United States. He gave up Soviet claims to Turkish territory and reestablished diplomatic ties with Greece and Israel. At the same time, he lifted the more fearsome qualities of the police state in the USSR and the countries of Eastern Europe.

For his part, President Eisenhower was at least inclined to follow up the end of the Korean War by responding positively to Malenkov. But he was checked by his secretary of state. A stern, moralistic, religion-invoking man, John Foster Dulles demanded that the captive peoples of Eastern Europe be liberated before the United States became friendlier with the USSR. The Soviets rejected Dulles's demand, and Premier Malenkov's position was weakened for being "soft on America." Meanwhile, Senator McCarthy was growing increasingly violent in his denunciations of "Commies, Commie lovers, and unwitting tools of the Kremlin," a catchall net, wide enough to cover any who disagreed with him. The matter was aggravated by American prisoners of war in Korea, who were subjected to intense physical and mental pressure. Some made broadcasts or signed petitions condemning the United States and capitalism. A very few chose to live in China after the armistice. Although psychiatrists said that the turncoats had been "brainwashed" and were not acting freely, many Americans safely at home found their attitude outrageous and even downright treasonous.

It was a difficult time for a U.S. president to try to alter the course of events and history. But there is a belief that great difficulties create great leaders, and that such circumstances made Winston Churchill a towering figure of the twentieth century. In any event, Malenkov's policies of liberalization toward the Communist-bloc countries backfired with East Berliners violently demanding faster and greater concessions. Spurred on by American broadcasts hinting that the liberation of the captive nations was at hand, the revolt spread to other East German cities and threatened to move into other Eastern European countries as well. At that point, Soviet tanks smashed the revolt in East Berlin and other East German cities.

Despite the briefness of this period of relaxation, the end of the Korean War and Stalin's death together with a new cast of international characters ended a chapter in the Cold War. The men who followed Stalin—Malenkov, Khrushchev, Brezhnev—were as fiercely USSR-first as the old dictator. But they were free of the worst of the persecution mania that had driven Stalin to imprison millions and kill hundreds of thousands. Korea had also demonstrated that the vital interests of the United States and the USSR could be touched and tested without automatically leading to an atomic nightmare. Finally, Korea contained the elements of conflict in the Soviet-Chinese alliance that would bring about greatly changed conditions in the Cold War.

Harrison Salisbury, a longtime observer of the Soviet Union, has argued that one of Stalin's reasons for encouraging a North Korean invasion of South Korea was to weaken China's as well as America's power in Asia. Stalin had not counted on U.S. or U.N. intervention. Instead, according to Salisbury, he expected that with his chosen man, Kim Il Sung, solidly entrenched on China's flank, Mao would be more vulnerable to Soviet pressure. Although the Sino-Soviet discord was concealed for most of the 1950s, in Salisbury's view the Korean War contributed to a breakdown of unity in the Communist camp, just as it did on the Western side.

The United States
and China

When the Korean War started in June 1950, Mao Tse-tung had been in power less than one year. It had taken him more than twenty years to get there, and those years had been spent fighting or fleeing. Given a choice, Mao probably would have preferred not to fight the Americans—at least not when he did.

Among the victorious nations of World War II, China had been at war the longest by far. Its struggles with the Japanese dated back to the 1920s. In 1931, Japan overran and detached Manchuria, and set up a puppet emperor. From 1937 onward, China was locked in a full-scale war with Japan. In addition, Nationalists and Communists had fought an on-off civil war since the 1920s.

For Americans, the Chinese had many faces, often wildly contradictory. On the one hand, there was art, culture, and medicine, thousands of years old; Confucian philosophy; and a wall—called the Great Wall—that had no equal in history. On the other hand, there was the more familiar and less respected image of Chinese restaurants and laundrymen; Chinatown; and the comic strip "Terry and the Pirates." In its relations with China, the United States had been equally contradictory, sending Christian missionaries to teach love and meekness and armed troops to exact obedience. In World War II, the names that Americans associated with China were Generalissimo Chiang Kai-shek and his glamorous wife; and the U.S. generals, Vinegar Joe Stilwell and Claire Chennault of the Flying Tigers. China was in most respects an unknown land.

With the largest population in the world and its slow entry into the modern world of science, engineering, and communications, it was easy to pass China off as a slumbering giant. In fact, there was little slumbering what with periodic invasions by the Japanese, Russians, and others; the forays of regional warlords; and finally, the contest between the Communists and the Nationalists. The Communists had suffered disastrous defeats by the Nationalists in 1927 and 1928. In the early 1930s, they began a six-thousand-mile retreat into the interior of the country under the most difficult circumstances, thereby avoiding total annihilation. The retreat, under the direction of Mao, who was at serious odds with Stalin, became known as the Long March. For its survivors, it became a medal of distinction. In 1937, the Nationalists and Communists declared a truce in order to fight the Japanese. But each side knew that eventually there would be a fight to the finish. Mao Tse-tung, having survived battles within the Chinese Communist party as well as against the Nationalists, was determined to win the next round.

The Russians, as the first people to establish a Communist —or, as they called it, a socialist—state, believed they were the rightful leaders of a worldwide revolution. Karl Marx had maintained that the new socialist states would be based on workers' societies, and Lenin had declared the need for a "dictatorship of the proletariat." After Lenin's death, Stalin pressed his ideas on the Chinese Communists and sent political and military advisers to help enforce his view. The near-destruction of the Communists by Chiang Kai-shek was, in Mao's opinion, a result of following Stalin's orders too closely. Mao's independence earned him Stalin's hostility, and the hostility of Stalin's successors. Nevertheless, Mao stuck to his decision that the Chinese revolution required its own national personality, one based on the peasants.

Wanting to run his own show was not peculiar to Mao. Battles between Soviet Communists and Communist leaders in other countries have waxed and waned over a sixty-year period. Although Communist ideology denies it, the conflicts generally are based on older enmities that predate Communism and persist despite the supposed common goal of universal socialism. In practice, when the Russians were too powerful to resist, the national leaderships gave way. Protracted stubbornness brought a summons to Moscow for disciplining, "reeducation," or sterner treatment. On the other hand, when national leaders found themselves less dependent on the Soviets, for example during periods of relaxation in the Cold War, they spoke out more strongly and openly. While maintaining their allegiance to Marx and Lenin, they then disputed the correctness of the Soviet chiefs in dictating to them. This development has continued to the present day.

Mao's reliance on the peasants proved well-founded, and the Communists increased their hold over the countryside. As for Chiang Kai-shek, the war against Japan revealed the weakness of his forces. Japan's surrender was a signal for the civil war to resume. General Marshall spent a year in China in 1946 trying to arrange a coalition between the two sides. But his mission failed, as did other efforts. Interestingly, at Potsdam, the Soviets supported Chiang as the national leader behind whom the Chinese presumably could unify. When the Soviet army evacuated Manchuria in 1946, they did so in a way that permitted Nationalist troops to contest the Communists for control. Stalin had not forgotten his feud with Mao, although it was not interpreted that way at the time. Nevertheless, the Chinese Communists were too strong. As they moved forward, the Nationalists fell back. China experts in the U.S. State Department and in other Foreign Offices predicted that Chiang's days were numbered.

Early in 1949, moving down from northern and central China, the Communists crossed the Yangtze River into South China and completely routed the Nationalists. Most damaging to the Nationalists was the loss or black-market sale to the Communists of great quantities of military equipment supplied by the United States. Chiang Kai-shek withdrew to Formosa, claiming that he would continue the battle for liberation of mainland China from there.

Whatever his weakness on the battlefield, Chiang had powerful backers in the United States, consisting of prominent political, military, and business leaders. Known as the China Lobby, its members were moved by a combination of missionary spirit, violent anti-Communism, and economic opportunism. Any criticism of Chiang or a positive statement about Mao brought abuse and suspicion on those who spoke out. When the Truman administration moved to stop further aid to the ousted Nationalists, Chiang's supporters in Congress rose in furious protest. Other countries and people have had powerful backing in the U.S. Congress, often as a result of legislators with ties to those countries: Ireland, Italy, Israel, Poland, Greece, Czechoslovakia, to name some of the more prominent cases. But none of the Nationalist Chinese backers were Chinese, although Congressman Walter Judd had been a missionary in China. That did not stop the evangelical free-enterprise oratory of men like Senator Kenneth Wherry of Nebraska, who declared while Chiang was still on the mainland: "With God's help we will lift Shanghai up and up, ever up, until it is just like Kansas City." Senator William Knowland defended President Chiang so passionately that newspaper editorial cartoonists nicknamed him "the Senator from Formosa."

Secretary of State Acheson tried to set the record straight by releasing a long document, running more than one thousand pages. It was called the "White Paper." It blamed the Nationalists' defeat on their own actions, not on U.S. failure to supply them with military or economic assistance. The China Lobby was not convinced or appeased. Its members condemned the "White Paper" as "a whitewash of a wishful, do-nothing policy which has succeeded only in placing Asia in danger of Soviet conquest."

Through their power in Congress, Chiang's supporters were able to block recognition of Mao Tse-tung's government. Within days after proclamation of the People's Republic of China, on October 1, 1949, Secretary of State Acheson announced that the new government would not be recognized because it had not met traditional American conditions. Nevertheless, many within the State Department argued for recognition, and without the Korean War, it probably would have come before too long.

In those days, most Americans thought of Moscow and Peking as inseparable allies. The "Bamboo Curtain" was considered an Asian version of the "Iron Curtain" in Europe. And the outbreak of the Korean War reinforced the notion that the United States was fighting an airtight Sino-Soviet bloc. In fact, the situation was far different. The USSR had kept an ambassador in Nanking assigned to the Nationalist government in 1949 after many other nations had abandoned Chiang. And although completely concealed from public view, negotiations for aid from Russia dragged on for two months after Mao came to power. The economic assistance to China was important, but compared with the Marshall Plan, it was extremely modest; in addition, the Soviets demanded and received repayment in full.

If the majority of Americans accepted a view of the Chinese Communists as devils, there were others who saw Mao and his followers as "agrarian reformers"—peasants and farmers who wanted a better distribution of the land, nothing more. As events were to show, this was a romantic and naïve view. In 1949, the Chinese Communists were bona fide revolutionaries, far more so than their Soviet counterparts. With a great underdeveloped land and inferior industrial capabilities, Mao was convinced that severe dictatorial methods were needed to move his country the way he wanted. He was a dedicated supporter also of "wars of national liberation" in Asia and Africa. On the other hand, the Chinese Communist intention to take Formosa was hardly a telltale sign of overall aggressiveness. Both Nationalists and Communists agreed that Formosa was part of China. Only the native Formosans, or Taiwanese as they are known to the Chinese, wanted no part of either. Since they were not in a position to assert their will, there was little they could do. Whether Mao had serious *territorial* ambitions beyond Taiwan, as distinguished from a Chinese "sphere of influence" in Asia, is open to question. Yet because of Korea, the Chinese Communists were branded as aggressors, an outlaw nation not fit to be admitted to the United Nations.

In examining the Cold War, the issue is not whether the Chinese Communists were ruthless in seeking to change their society, even at the cost of killing hundreds of thousands who opposed them. They were ruthless, but that scarcely put them in a class by themselves compared with some non-Communist members of the U.N. Within China itself, the Communists were not the first oppressors. For centuries, the Chinese had been subjected to foreign invasion, occupation, and demands for tribute. Warlords had been equally indifferent to the sufferings of the peasants. Nor had the experience with Chiang led them to believe that friendship and alliance with the Western democracies would improve their lot. The question, instead, is whether the Chinese Communists forced the United States into an eastern extension of the Cold War, or whether the United States was drawn in by the force of events.

For the Chinese Communists, newly established in government, the Soviet Union was the available ally despite some poor experiences during the previous thirty years. But their relations with the United States were no worse at the beginning of 1949 than those of other nondemocratic nations with whom the United States maintained relations. A proud group, the new Chinese leaders might have believed that the China-first policies of Mao gradually would be accepted in the West, even if not welcomed. But a string of events, beginning with the unusual strength of the China Lobby in the United States, made it otherwise. Finally, the war in Korea, in which the Chinese probably were only marginally involved at the start, set the seal on the history of U.S.-Chinese relations for the next quarter of a century.

Round Two: Vietnam

The leaders of great powers pride themselves on being realists. They understand that they exercise power because they can enforce their will, generally by a combination of military, political, and economic means. But we also know that in the post–World War II period, both Democratic and Republican presidents wanted to believe that America was a world leader because it was democratic, moral, and concerned with the well-being of other nations. In contrast, they found their rivals in Communist Russia and Communist China precisely the opposite.

When Americans spoke of the Free World versus the Communist World, they also meant good versus bad.

The Korean War ended without victory for either side. The Eisenhower administration believed the Democrats had handled the war poorly, but they agreed that President Truman had been right to step in on the side of the South Koreans. The fact that South Korean President Syngman Rhee was a dictator was less important than the fact that he was a staunch anti-Communist. Americans explained their support for dictators by saying that once those countries were free of the Communist menace, they would become more democratic.

President Eisenhower spoke of morality in domestic policy and in foreign affairs and set himself apart from "politicians" who were not as high-minded. But it was John Foster Dulles, Eisenhower's secretary of state, who put himself squarely on the side of the angels. Again and again he made a black-and-white distinction between the Communist World and the Free World. Dulles preached a muscular brand of Christianity. He believed that by forming a network of global alliances, patterned on NATO, the Free World led by the U.S. could defeat the atheistic Communists. Without openly advocating military action against the USSR and mainland China, he condemned the status quo of the world in which Communist governments were allowed to continue in power.

Dulles was almost as stern in his denunciations of neutrality as he was in condemning Communism. It was as though he were unaware of the long tradition of U.S. neutrality, nonalignment, and nonintervention when he chided leaders of neutralist nations for not siding with the United States. His special targets were Josip Broz Tito of Yugoslavia, Gamal Abdel Nasser of Egypt, and Jawaharlal Nehru of India—three men completely different in background, geographical concerns, and long-term goals. Tito was an avowed Marxist on the outs with the Soviets; Nasser and Nehru considered themselves Socialists, but Egypt was a military dictatorship and India the world's largest democracy. Each man was highly popular with his people. What they shared was a determination to set their own national courses, independent of the wishes of the United States and the USSR. They also believed that by bringing together other nations that wished to stay out of big-power alliances, they could exert influence on both superpowers. They became the first leaders of what became known as the Third World.

During his term as secretary of state from 1953 until his death in 1959, Dulles tried unsuccessfully to bully Tito, Nasser, and Nehru to side with the United States against the Soviet Union and China. For the most part he antagonized them and created anti-American feeling. Countries such as Pakistan, Iran, and Thailand followed the U.S. lead because they felt themselves threatened militarily. In Africa, Dulles was unable to build even the semblance of a U.S. alliance as new nations emerged.

Dulles's refusal to accept neutrality as a way of life for many nations was coupled with U.S. inability to compel most nations to do its bidding. The same, incidentally, was true for the Soviet Union. What did the most, however, to unravel the high-minded, high-sounding global aims of the United States were a series of events in another of those remote, little-known places. This time it was Indochina.

Even as the war in Korea ended, the one in Indochina pitting the French against the Communist-led forces of Ho Chi Minh intensified. The French had been losing ground steadily in their efforts to maintain an empire in Indochina against the popular nationalist leader Ho Chi Minh. In the middle of 1954, the French were backed into a small, strategically indefensible pocket at Dien Bien Phu. Recognizing the hopelessness of the situation too late, the French government pleaded desperately for American intervention. The U.S. Air Force chief of staff was ready to respond. He proposed dropping a few small nuclear bombs around Dien Bien Phu and having the French march out, heads high and flags flying. President Eisenhower was not convinced that it would be so clean and neat. He leaned toward a

(top) Heads of five important neutralist countries at a conference in New York in 1960. Left to right: Prime Minister Nehru of India, President Nkrumah of Ghana, President Nasser of the United Arab Republic, President Sukarno of Indonesia, and President Tito of Yugoslavia. (bottom) Cuban Premier Castro speaks to a crowd during a visit to Chile.

nonnuclear air strike, but he wanted foreign support. In the end, lack of backing by the Congress or the British persuaded the administration to hold back. It marked another of those episodes that has been debated as to what might have been, had the decision been otherwise.

Dien Bien Phu fell. The French and Viet Minh, as the Ho Chi Minh forces were called, negotiated an armistice. But even as the French retreated from Vietnam, the United States began to be pulled in, first through economic and military assistance, then with military advisers. Under the pretense of strengthening the democratic forces of South Vietnam against the totalitarianism of Communist North Vietnam, the United States steadily increased its fighting forces. By 1968, they exceeded half a million men. In contrast to Korea, there was no United Nations command, and only minimal support from U.S. allies. Also the "democratic forces" of Ngo Dinh Diem, Nguyen Cao Ky, and Nguyen Van Thieu were unconvincing as champions of freedom and democracy. The goal of winning the hearts and minds of the South and North Vietnamese people against the Communist Viet Cong and North Vietnamese forces proved futile. To the embarrassment of the Americans, it was the United States and South Vietnam, not the Communists, who opposed free elections. This time it was painfully clear that Ho Chi Minh would win.

Even more demoralizing to U.S. self-esteem was the realization that the immense technological superiority of U.S. forces was of little use in defeating the Communist opposition. Patient, resourceful, ready to sacrifice tens of thousands of lives, the Viet Cong were masters of guerrilla warfare. Not for them were the pitched battles the United States sought. Instead, they melted away before a trap was sprung and turned up to harass and fight elsewhere. The frustration was enormous. In World Wars I and

II, the United States had battled the world's major powers and emerged victorious. In the Korean War, Americans had salvaged some pride in grinding far larger Chinese armies to a standstill while holding back their Sunday nuclear punch. But in Vietnam, the United States was bedeviled—yes, and finally defeated —by a small Asian nation.

At home, most of the American military chiefs were furious at being humiliated on the battlefield. Given their way, they were convinced that by mining North Vietnamese ports, bombing industrial targets in China, and if necessary, using some small nuclear weapons, they could bring the war to a speedy end. They were never given a chance to test their theory. All the presidents, from Eisenhower to Ford, knew that the sheer destructive power of the United States could wipe out all Vietnam. But they also realized that bombing China would bring the Chinese in full tilt, and that the Russians might be sucked in as well. The risk of a thermonuclear war was too great for a U.S. chief executive to gamble with a few "tactical nuclear weapons" in hopes that the other side would not raise the stakes.

Among the U.S. population, the Vietnam War had never been popular. Initially a majority supported the government and believed that victory was in sight, that there was light at the end of the tunnel. The Vietnam War had started with one strike against it. It was a continuation of France's losing fight. Furthermore, it lacked a dramatic beginning—such as Soviet-made tanks racing across the Thirty-eighth Parallel. In addition, while most Americans realize that war is not at all glamorous, Vietnam seemed especially dirty and distasteful. In the early 1960s when Kennedy was president, there was a degree of patriotism and understandable concern by families of men in Vietnam. As the war dragged on, disillusion deepened. Americans involved in

[69]

*Anti-war protests in the U.S. grew more and
more widespread. Here, a contingent of Vietnam
veterans takes part in a 1972 protest march.*

napalm bombing of civilian villages and acts of atrocity at My Lai did not square with the notion of the way the United States fought a war. The young people of the country became louder and angrier in their opposition to the war. At first, it sharpened the conflict and will of Americans on both sides. The "hawks" denounced the "doves" as cowards who did not want to fight and defend their country, and the sometimes uncritical support of the Viet Cong by these antiwar Americans unsettled other Americans who were not "hawks" but did not like cheering the Communist enemy. With the passage of futile months and years, support for the war dwindled to a small, hard-core minority. The South Vietnamese army, despite years of training, assistance, and billions of dollars in equipment, could not stand up to its enemies.

President Lyndon Johnson had won a landslide election in 1964 against Senator Barry Goldwater, who had frightened people into believing that he would start unloading nuclear weapons if elected. By mid-1968, Johnson's commitment of 500,000 men to a war that was still not won had made him so unpopular that he retired rather than risk defeat by seeking reelection. By the irony that brought General Eisenhower to the presidency in 1952 to get the country out of Korea, it was Richard Nixon, a symbol of anti-Communism and anti-Maoism, who succeeded Johnson and negotiated an end to Vietnam.

In 1975 when the last American troops evacuated South Vietnam, the Cold War as it had taken shape originally was done and over. Most of the predictions of how one superpower or the other would fall because of its rotted system had failed to come true. Most striking was what had happened between old friends and old enemies, as the Cold War wound down and passed into history.

[71]

Call It Détente

By 1976, the bitterest foe of the Union of Soviet Socialist Republics and of the People's Republic of China was not the United States of America, but each other.

In the United States, Communism was still regarded as a menace, but in the 1970s the criticisms of Washington coming from capitals of the Third World in Africa, Southeast Asia, and the Middle East outstripped those from Moscow and Peking.

In its fourth decade, the Nuclear Club now included Great Britain, China, France, and India in addition to the United States and USSR. Other nations such as Canada, the two Germanies, Sweden, Israel, and Taiwan were regarded as capable of producing nuclear weapons, if they had not already done so without testing them. And there were recurring stories that still other nations had obtained nuclear weapons, or had received standby guarantees to get them in the event of war.

From a positive standpoint, after thirty years no nation had used its nuclear arsenal against another, despite temptation and provocation. The longer the world went without a nuclear outburst, the better the chances that there would be none. But as long as there were no strong bans on using nuclear weapons, the possibility of a sudden thermonuclear disaster persisted. Furthermore, the chance of a smaller power lighting the fuse, rather than a superpower, gave Americans and Russians a common cause.

The Baruch Plan in 1946, named for Bernard Baruch, a U.S. elder statesman, represented the earliest attempt by one of the Big Two to put nuclear weapons off bounds. To Americans, the Baruch Plan to place nuclear weapons under international control seemed an unmistakably generous and peace-loving act. They doubted that the Soviets would have made the offer, if the Soviets had the only A-bombs in the world. But the Russians rejected the plan. Subsequent Soviet proposals, in turn, were rejected, as were those of other nations. Nevertheless, the United States and USSR realized that each country's national interest required something that went beyond "no-war, no-peace," "balance of terror," "mutual deterrence," or "containment."

The desire for mutual survival brought limited cooperation in trade and cultural relations while putting limits on nuclear weapon rattling. The two drew closer together, then sprang apart, like two dancers who approach but never touch. Each fresh attempt to reduce tension brought new phrases as well. The most recent one in 1976 was "détente." It was the latest try by each country to find a way to live and let live without yielding a strategic advantage to the other.

Inevitably, there were temptations to get one-up on the other, even while trying to relax tensions. The results were not always predictable. For example, the Soviet Union and the United States found themselves on the same side when the British and French, in cooperation with Israel, invaded Egypt in October 1956 to seize the Suez Canal. The USSR threatened London and Paris with nuclear bombardment if they did not withdraw from Egypt. President Eisenhower, with Election Day at hand and furious at not being consulted by the French and British, joined other nations in the U.N. in demanding British-French-Israeli withdrawal from Egypt.

The Suez invasion came only days before the most serious armed uprising in Eastern Europe faced by the Russians. But with the Western powers badly divided because of Suez, Soviet tanks crushed the revolt in Hungary without serious danger of outside interference. If there had been no Suez, would the United States have tried to check the Russians? No one knows. Short of using U.S. troops, the Russians probably would not have been deterred. We do know that in 1958, two years later, the United States put troops ashore in Lebanon at the invitation of the Lebanese president. Soviet threats without the backup of military force proved to be hollow.

In 1957, the USSR had beaten the United States in their race to place the first satellite in space. Their ability to do so signaled an important Soviet lead in the contest for an intercontinental ballistic missile (ICBM). An operational Soviet ICBM meant U.S. cities were within easy Soviet atomic reach. It sent a shock through America's allies. Would the United States still be willing to oppose the USSR now that American cities could be missile targets, they asked. Lebanon provided a partial answer, but a more definitive one came in Cuba.

In April 1961, a recently inaugurated President John F. Kennedy had suffered a disaster in his own backyard. An insurgent band of Cubans, trained and supplied by the U.S. Central Intelligence Agency, had invaded Cuba at the Bay of Pigs. The planning had begun during the final years of President Eisenhower's second term, but the degree of U.S. participation was not firmly fixed. The invasion turned into a rout. The population did not rise against Premier Fidel Castro, and the United States was left looking like an inept bungler.

Against this background, the Soviets thought they saw a rare opportunity to gain an important advantage vis-à-vis the Americans. After the Bay of Pigs, Khrushchev had tried to bully and frighten Kennedy at a meeting in Vienna. Shortly thereafter in August 1961, the Berlin Wall went up, daring the United States to do anything about it. Now, the Soviets reckoned, the United States would hesitate to turn loose its naval, air, and land forces without a clear and direct provocation. With the agreement of his ally Castro, Khrushchev secretly began constructing missile bases on Cuba, ninety miles from the U.S. mainland. By the time the secret was out and the U.N. might act, Khrushchev believed it would be too late to undo the deed. His calculations were wrong. Thanks to high-flying U-2 reconnaissance planes, Kennedy knew what was afoot. Before the Soviets could finish their installations, the United States demanded that they pull out. If necessary, the United States would go to war. The Soviets had struck too close to the bone. In an "eyeball to eyeball" confrontation between Khrushchev and Kennedy, Khrushchev blinked first and retreated.

But in the Cold War, today's victory was likely to be offset by tomorrow's defeat. Smaller nations, particularly those in the Third World, outside the orbit of the superpowers, found it possible to play one side against the other. In the Middle East, the Soviets discovered that their bailout of Egypt, after the United States and United Kingdom refused to finance the Aswan Dam in 1956, gave them a limited amount of credit, but not a lasting friendship. When President Sadat became angry with the Russians in 1971, he ordered them to withdraw their military advisers and technicians. The Soviets obeyed. Nevertheless in 1973, after the Israelis turned the tide against Egypt and Syria following an Arab surprise attack, the Soviets saved an Egyptian army by obliging the Israelis to agree to a cease-fire. Even that act did not spare the Soviets further rebuffs by the Egyptians in the months that followed.

Together with the Third World's greater awareness of its bargaining power with the United States and USSR came disagreements within the Eastern and Western alliances. The change in relations between the Soviet Union and the People's Republic of China was the more dramatic of the two. The liberalization in the USSR in 1956 following Nikita Khrushchev's denunciation of the dead hero-tyrant Stalin had tremendous shock effects among Communist countries. It led to violent demonstrations in Poland and to the overthrow of the government in Hungary. Only the strength of the Red Army put Hungarian Communists back in control. In China, Mao set himself firmly against friendlier relations with capitalist nations. He was convinced that the future of socialism in China, as well as his own fortunes, could be undercut by abandoning a revolutionary attitude. He set himself firmly against the Soviet leadership and increased his calls for "wars of national liberation" in Africa and Asia. For the Soviets, tolerating Marshal Tito's dissent was one matter; to allow a head-on challenge for international Communist leadership from Mao could shake the foundations of the Soviet system. The old Russian-Chinese enmities and rivalries for dominance in East Asia were far stronger than the ties of Marxist solidarity.

As a result, what had seemed to the West like a solid front between the Russians and the Chinese Communists began to show cracks. Starting in the late 1950s with the "code language" that only specialists in the State Department and other Foreign Offices could translate, the Sino-Soviet quarrel became more open, louder, and more insulting. By the mid-1960s, each was accusing the other of playing the capitalist game. Eventually the accusations grew to mutual condemnation of "revisionist renegade cliques," "social imperialists," and "subversives."

The Russian-Chinese feud opened the path to a remarkable shift in U.S. policy. In July 1971, Richard Nixon, a man who had built his reputation on an uncompromising opposition to international Communism, sent his national security adviser, Henry Kissinger, on a top-secret mission. Destination: Peking. Objective: to open relations between the People's Republic of China and the United States of America. While there had been periods of relaxation in U.S.-Soviet relations since World War II, with Communist China there had been only downs, no ups. Contacts between the two nations had been severely limited with virtually no trade or travel. The United States, it was repeated, was firmly and unwaveringly committed to its Nationalist Chinese allies on Taiwan. In the United Nations, the United States had repeatedly blocked admission of the Peking government, even after a majority of members wanted its admission. But by 1971, the United States accepted the inevitable, as the People's Republic of China was voted into the U.N. and the Republic of China (Taiwan) was voted out.

The full drama of the change of U.S. public opinion and official governmental policy came in February 1972. Amidst much fanfare at home and abroad, President Nixon journeyed to Peking. He stood on the Great Wall, exchanged toasts with the Chinese leaders, and sat side by side with Mao Tse-tung. Shortly thereafter, the two countries took the first steps toward normalizing relations by exchanging diplomatic representatives and expanding their trade. Meanwhile, the Chinese Nationalists on

Taiwan had become strong enough economically to carry on independently, despite dwindling diplomatic status. Contrary to predictions, two Chinas were coexisting.

Without admitting it openly, in the 1970s both China and Russia were competing for U.S. support against the other. When Gerald Ford became president, one of his early acts in 1975 was to visit both Peking and Moscow to reassure their leaders of friendly American intentions. In the past when new presidents took trips abroad, it was to buck up old friends or troubled allies. Now rivalry, hostility, even warlike gestures could still pit the United States against the USSR or the People's Republic of China. But America's unequivocal crusade against the twin apostles of international Communism had been put on the shelf.

Beyond Détente

Deep in space, 136 (219 km) miles from Planet Earth, an American general and a Russian colonel met and shook hands.

The meeting was not a science-fiction film or a chapter from a novel. It was an actual event, beamed by television, in July 1975, into the homes of hundreds of millions of people around the globe. Watching these spacemen float about, the similarities between American and Russian seemed far greater than their differences.

The Soviets had been first to put a man in space in 1961. It was a tremendous achievement for a nation that barely forty years earlier had been a feudal, agricultural society. But the United States, awakened at last to the unexpected scientific and engineering abilities of the Russians, had staged a gigantic come-from-behind effort and rocketed the first man to the moon.

By differing paths, the USSR and the United States of America had moved a long distance in their developments. George Kennan, one of America's outstanding experts on the Soviet Union, had predicted years ago that these two rivals would gradually come together. He had lived to see some of his predictions come true.

Admittedly the governments, the personal liberties, and the style of living in the United States and the Soviet Union are very different. While repressions and freedoms exist in both countries, they are not comparable. A purge or a blacklist in the United States during the worst of the McCarthy era in the 1950s could mean loss of employment and reputation, or even a prison term for contempt of Congress. But in terms of harshness, that is light-years distant from the prison camps, torture, and execution that millions of Soviet citizens suffered for opposition to the government. Physically, Red Square and Times Square are in no way alike. Culturally, Americans and Russians are treated to much different fare on television, in motion pictures, and in the books and newspapers that they read. Having said all that, in this last quarter of the twentieth century there are more similarities between the United States and the USSR than there were twenty years ago.

But, the reader may ask, even if the United States and USSR are moving ever so slowly toward each other, what has changed since the Cold War began, and how can we say it has ended?

Most important, both countries realize that war with the other must be avoided, if at all possible. Threats, slurs on the national reputation, even setbacks on the battlefield, they have agreed, are not cause for a thermonuclear war. Win some, lose some, but don't burn up the earth. Second, both recognize that the other has a security line which must not be crossed. At its extreme, this bars invasion or bombing. It also means exercising the greatest caution in using a neighboring country as a potential springboard for disrupting the other. Finally, there is a reluctant acceptance that many countries cannot be bought or bullied for more than short periods. The rise of a powerful oil cartel in the Middle East, led by Iran and the Arab nations, was not due to the prompting of the United States, the USSR, or China. Saudi Arabia and Iran were considered U.S. allies; Iraq, Syria, and Libya friends of the Soviets. But oil-country interests, not ideology, won the day and they do not seem subject to veto by a "great power."

In the early postwar years, the allies of the United States and USSR toed the line with little public protest. Marshal Tito of Yugoslavia defied the Russians and survived. He finally prospered, but for years he was an exception. Then Fidel Castro did the same to the United States. Still, the superpowers were not toothless tigers. In 1968, liberalization of Czechoslovakia swelled to a point where the Soviets could see a tidal wave engulfing Eastern Europe. Soviet troops moved, as they had against Hungary in 1956, and the new sparks of freedom in Czechoslovakia were snuffed out. In Chile, a Marxist government, democratically come to power, alarmed the United States to a point where the Central Intelligence Agency helped overthrow President Allende in 1973 for a more amenable leader.

Chairman Mao, until his death in 1976, was the oldest, most experienced, and wiliest of the world's leaders in maintaining power during decades of change and challenge. In 1956 and 1957 during a brief liberalization period, he seemed to herald a new day of many opinions in China when he said, "Let a hundred flowers bloom." Later, too late for many, that slogan turned out to be a test, or a trap, to find out who was disloyal. Almost a decade later, Mao caught others of his followers off guard by launching the Cultural Revolution. It unleashed the force of young people against government and army bureaucrats. The Cultural Revolution unseated Mao's rivals and critics and left him in undisputed control, although for a time Mao himself was threatened by the new revolutionary zeal. Outside China, however, even in countries on its border and those with large Chinese populations, Mao could not enforce obedience.

As for the United States and the USSR, despite occasionally successful crackdowns, they were reminded constantly of their

Soviet tanks rumbled into Prague for swift occupation in 1968, when the Czechs went too far in liberalizing their Communist government.

limitations. In Europe—east and west of what was known as the Iron Curtain—Communists declared limited independence. In Romania, France, Italy, and Spain, leaders say that Communism is international, but first it flies the national banner. A hundred flowers may not bloom, but a dozen shades of red and pink are a growing possibility.

In the United States, the once popular term "Free World," used to describe its allies arrayed in solid democratic ranks against Communism, has become badly frayed. Some non-Communist nations are as harsh or harsher than Communist nations in demanding their citizens' obedience. This country's staunchest and oldest friends, France, Britain, and Canada, are critical, defiant, and even hostile to America. In the United Nations General Assembly, the United States is hard pressed to get respectable support for any resolution it introduces. The days of the automatic U.S. majority are memories.

Domestically, there have been changes in the United States and USSR as well. By all accounts, the worst days of Stalin's terror are absent. Dissent is still risky, but rarely fatal. Travel, cultural, scientific, and economic exchange, and even emigration have opened the Soviet Union to a much greater degree. Meanwhile, in the United States, recent presidents have been more inclined to use national security to justify the invasion of individual rights, sometimes secretly and illegally. So far in the United States a combination of the media—press, TV, and radio—and the opposition party have pulled the pendulum back from an extreme swing, but it is disturbing.

So we say the Cold War is dead. The old contest in which each side tried to pull down the other by all means short of head-to-head war is over. Sworn enemies of yesterday are invited to come closer. The United States and USSR find each has a major stake in having the other stay in business. If one superpower fell, it would not make life easier for the other. Instead, it would probably compound the difficulties that exist, by substituting unpredictable dangers for known ones.

Are we, then, at the beginning of an era of peace and goodwill?

The odds are that the answer is no. The great powers continue to choose up sides in the Middle East. But they do not start the wars and they can stop them only with great difficulty. Americans have become accustomed to saying a major war is unthinkable, that a thermonuclear war would end civilization as we know it. But for many nations, war is not only thinkable, it is still the most practical way of handling a dispute. It can be a good way of settling your neighbor's hash, and it is an effective means of putting down domestic opponents and gaining greater power. As the Chinese have pointed out, a thermonuclear war that killed hundreds of millions of people would still leave millions of Chinese survivors.

In the countries of Africa, the Middle East, Asia, and Latin America, there are continuing rumbles and upheavals, like a volcano that has had a spectacular eruption but has not settled into a peaceful part of the landscape. In Cuba, Castro has thwarted more than one assassination attempt. He has consolidated his support after nearly twenty years in power and carved out a new role for himself as an exporter of revolutions to Angola and other parts of Africa. Events that were once viewed from Washington and Moscow as *their* competition for the loyalties of peoples of the Third World now occur with only marginal reference to the superpowers. The real winners and losers are neither Russians nor Americans. And the experts are as confounded as most others in predicting how the scales will be arranged in the next balance of power.

The fact is that as the political world broke loose from the two power poles of Washington and Moscow, it did not form around two, three, or four new ones. In Western Europe, the prospects for a true United States of Europe rise and fall. When Western Europeans feel threatened, they draw more tightly together. The threat of outside danger has historically persuaded those threatened to band together. The Cold War repeatedly demonstrated the truth of that proposition. Politicians in all countries during the 1950s and 1960s used the Cold War as both a defensive or offensive weapon. The British are now members of the Common Market, which is a plus for unification, but unless member nations surrender some of their political sovereignty, there will be no united Western Europe. The future of Eastern Europe is cloudy, too. As the Soviet Union loosened its grip to a degree on those countries, they neither came together voluntarily nor moved impulsively toward the West. To the extent allowed them, the Eastern European countries examine their interests from a national viewpoint, not an ideological or new power-bloc one.

In Africa and Latin America, the organization of states to which countries on those continents belong is a promise rather than a prophecy of soon-to-come unity. As for Asia, it is a continent of many different civilizations rather than one of organizations and alliances.

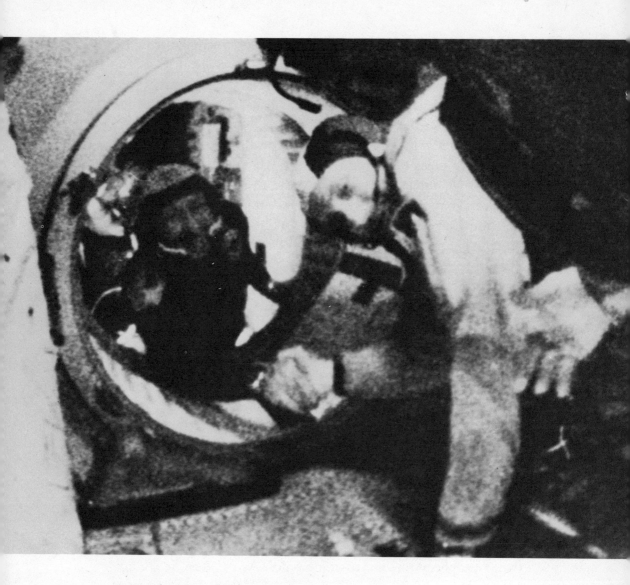

*A handshake in space between a U.S.
astronaut and Soviet cosmonaut during
the July 1975 joint Earth-orbit mission.*

An unexpected postscript to the Cold War is that the nations of Western Europe, after years of railing at the United States for its interference in their internal affairs, now complain of American indifference. They question the United States' will to oppose the Soviets.

For the United States and the USSR there is less incentive now to go to war with each other or with anyone else, and greater risks of runaway conflicts. So in 1975, we saw them signing a declaration in Helsinki that accepts existing borders in Europe, asserts the need for better relations among nations, and proclaims the rights of individuals. These old enemies of the Cold War now walk a tightrope and try not to pile up newer and more costly weapons beyond what their economies can handle. At the same time, they are wary that the other side will get a military jump and be tempted to try a major power play.

As 1984 draws closer, the world that George Orwell portrayed in the novel of that title has not been realized—a world in which personal rights and freedom had virtually vanished. "Big Brother" was everywhere. But in another book, *Animal Farm,* Orwell told a fable of a society in which all the animals were equal, but some were "more equal" than others. To be "more equal" is the goal of people and nations east, west, north, and south. So the race goes on with unabashed force. And the hope that détente will finally lead to peace on earth has drawn this comment from a present-day animal-world observer, "When the lion and the lamb lie down together, I want to be the lion."

Index

[89]